The Investigator

Allan Ramsay

Garland Publishing, Inc., New York

1971

AC
7
·R34
1971

Bibliographical note:
this facsimile has been made from a
copy in the Yale University Library
(Beinecke Im R149 762J)

Library of Congress Catalog Card Number: 72-112216

Printed in U.S.A.

THE

INVESTIGATOR.

Containing the following TRACTS:

I. ON RIDICULE.

II. ON ELIZABETH CANNING.

III. ON NATURALIZATION.

IV. ON TASTE.

Δοξα μεν ανθροποισι κακον μεγα, Πειρα δ᾽ αριστον.
THEOGNIS.

LONDON:
Printed in the Year MDCCLXII.

A N

ESSAY

ON

RIDICULE.

Jocandi recte sapere est principium et fons.

L O N D O N:
Printed for A. MILLAR in the Strand.
MDCCLIII.

Advertisement.

THE following Essay was written by a man of business, for
his winter evenings amusement, and
belongs to a series of tracts, all tending
to shew the usefulness and necessity of
experimental reasoning in philological and moral enquiries.

As he is but a young trader in
the way of literature, and his goods
of a fabric somewhat new, he does
not think it prudent to risque much
of his stock upon one bottom. From
the returns of approbation, which he
shall receive from this small venture,
he will be better enabled to judge

what

what the demand is at market; and
will then know, with some degree of
certainty, whether he ought to export
any more of the same kind; whether
he should work up the materials,
still on his hands, in another fashion;
or, which is most likely to happen,
whether he had not better reserve
them altogether for home consump-
tion.

C O N-

CONTENTS.

PART I.

PART II.

AN ESSAY ON RIDICULE.

PART I.

SECTION I.

AFTER a curious fubject has been unfuccefsfully treated by philofophers, poets, phyficians, and divines of reputation, it might feem prefumptuous in one to attempt it, whofe neceffary ftudies have been of a nature little connected with deep erudition, and who has but few hours of leifure, from his ordinary occupation, to put together the little he may have accidentally pickt up; were it not known,

B

at

PART I. at the fame time, that many valuable and furprifing difcoveries have accrued to mankind by the means of thofe from whom they were leaft to be expected. It is a trite obfervation, that printing was difcover'd by a foldier, and gun-powder by a monk; from which, and many other inftances, we may conclude, that the moft extraordinary inventions were rather the effect of chance and fubfequent trial, than of any profound forethought and contrivance.

The queftion, *whether Ridicule be a teft of truth*, is one of thofe which have divided the learned for fome years paft, without producing any thing fatisfactory, for or againft it; and if I fhould in the following fheets caft any new light upon the fubject, it is by means not unlike thofe of the difcoverer of gun-powder. He felt, when perhaps his reflection was otherwife employed, that this compofition had an uncommon force and quicknefs, called to mind what were its ingredients, and was only the hiftorian of his crucible.

Thofe who have already handled the fubject of Ridicule, have taken a very different method,

method, and, inftead of examining what it was compofed of, have not fo much as fettled, with any precifion, what the thing was which one party fo much extolled, and the other fo much depreciated.

Lord SHAFTSBURY, who, by his recommending Ridicule as a teft of truth, firft gave rife to this controverfy, expreffes himfelf fo varioufly, that it is as hard to guefs what he means to recommend, as upon what grounds. In his *Letter concerning Enthufiafm,* he oppofes it to formality, gravity, and melancholly, and calls it chearfulnefs, pleafantry, and good humour. Chearfulnefs is certainly an excellent quality in itfelf, and a difpofition of mind very proper for thofe who are to enter into any enquiry; but how it fhould any way be a teft of truth, more than a teft of gold, wine, filk, or other valuable commodity, it is difficult to conceive. In his *Effay on the Freedom of Wit and Humour,* where one expects to fee fomething more explicit, he rather feems to retract what he had fo warmly afferted; fpeaks of bounds and limitations to this teft of truth; hints at *a kind of defenfive raillery*

B 2   which

PART which is, as he explains it, some evasive me-
I. thod to keep truth, when discovered, from
certain persons. And altho' he had said in
his *Letter on Enthusiasm* *, *'Tis only in a free
nation, such as ours, that imposture has no
privilege, and that neither the credit of a
court, the power of a nobility, nor the awful-
ness of a church, can give her protection, and
hinder from being arraign'd in every shape
and appearance:* yet, in his *Essay on the
Freedom of Wit and Humour*, he jumbles
raillery, burlesque, and ridicule together,
and makes them the necessary language of
slavery †.

Non tali auxilio nec defensoribus istis——

As this very ingenious nobleman has been
commonly looked upon as the great patron
and supporter of Ridicule, I thought it incumbent upon me to point out in a few
words, how he has, or rather how he has
not treated it. Those who want to see a
more full examination of what his lordship
has advanced upon that head, will find it in

* Sect. II. near the beginning.
† Sect. IV. at the end.

a book

a book of *Essays* lately published, in opposition to his opinions in general *. But altho' I agree with the writer of those *Essays* in many of his remarks upon what Lord SHAFTSBURY has advanced concerning Ridicule; yet I shall take the liberty to dissent from him with regard to the subject itself; which I shall endeavour to prove to be what his Lordship at first asserted; one of *the tests of truth* (by its detection of falshood) and, as such, to be indulged without any limitation.

I am extremely sensible how difficult it is, even for the best writers, to convey their ideas with certainty by the means of general terms only. I shall therefore, in the prosecution of this work, endeavour to ascertain my meaning by the help of examples; so that, if I should happen to mean nothing to the purpose, (a thing very common among essay writers) it will be immediately apparent.

Had the celebrated writers who have exercised their pens upon the different sides of

---

* *Essays on the Characteristicks*, by JOHN BROWN, M, A. second edition.

this

PART this controverfy, ~~taken~~ to the tract here
I. pointed out, to wit, the examination of the
various examples of Ridicule, as they really ex-
ift in the works of men of acknowledged wit;
it is fcarce poffible but that they muft, long
e'er now, have come to a better underftanding. They could not have fpent much time
in the fcrutiny, without obferving, that there
are two forts of Ridicule; one of which is
employed in difcuffing propofitions, or matters of enquiry; and another, which has
manner and actions for its province. A
complaifance both for the vulgar language,
and for that which has been ufed by the beft
authors, obliges ~~one~~ to call both thefe things
by the name of Ridicule; tho' it will appear,
that their nature and properties are very different. I fhall therefore treat of them fe-
parately, beginning with that kind which is
employed in matters of enquiry; becaufe it
is the moft important in itfelf, and becaufe
it is that which gave rife to this controverfy;
being the only kind of Ridicule which can
fo much as pretend to be admitted as a teft
of truth.

Whatever then may hereafter befal the
other, this Ridicule may be defin'd, *the art*
of

of shewing that to be ridiculous which is ima- Sect. *gined to be so.* Perhaps I shall be told by I. some body, that this is the proper office of reason and argument. Whoever he be, I most heartily agree with him; having long thought that those advocates for Ridicule, who set it in opposition to reason, did its cause very little honour or service. I likewise join with the author of the *Essays on the Characteristicks,* in placing Ridicule among the modes of eloquence; but as he has chosen to separate eloquence from argument, I must endeavour to reconcile them, before I can hope to have Ridicule received as a test of truth; a praise, which is certainly due to argument alone.

SEC-

SECTION II.

PART
I.

THE Essay writer, in his division of the several kinds of composition, has assigned to argument the province of convincing by reality; and to eloquence, that of persuading by fictitious appearances. That is, that eloquence or oratory is, some how or other, the art of dazling or deceiving the understanding.

I do not profess in this Essay, as he has done in those he has published, to criticise the opinions of any author, except where my subject calls upon me; else I should perhaps be able to show, that what he advances, with regard to eloquence, might very well pass for a satire upon publick speaking in general, and upon that from the pulpit in particular. Indeed, to do him justice, he does not continue long in that opinion; but having sufficiently decried eloquence, in order to condemn Ridicule as one of its accomplices, he afterwards makes it amends, by acknowledging that eloquence is of the most excellent sort, when it is found-

ed

ed upon argument drawn from the real ex-
istence of things; so that there is no difficulty in concluding, that what he before said of eloquence in general, is only true of false eloquence.

But there is nothing in all this learned perplexity about *eloquence* and *argument*, *conviction* and *perswasion*, *judgment*, *passion* and *imagination*, but what may be easily unravel'd; provided we do not suffer ourselves to be intangled in other people's opinions, but examine into the nature of the subject itself. I will therefore enter upon it as if it had never been touched before; at the same time with that brevity which becomes an episode, and an episode which perhaps is very little necessary.

Eloquence is the art of convincing and perswading. These two properties of eloquence do not so much denote two different kinds of it, as the two different purposes to which it may be applied. This will appear from an enquiry into the proper meaning and application of the words, and likewise from the practice of the best orators.

When

PART
I.

When any opinion is to be examined, or any affertion to be proved, then the fole aim of oratory is to convince. When any action is to be performed, or let alone, then the aim of oratory is to perfuade. We fay, *perfuade to a thing*, in this latter cafe ; and *convince of a thing*, in the former. Whenever a truth is to be inveftigated, the underftanding alone is concerned ; and therefore eloquence applies itfelf to the underftanding only, with intention to convince. Whenever an action is to be promoted, eloquence applies itfelf to the two fprings of human action, the underftanding and the paffions, alternately ; endeavouring both to convince and perfuade. From this neceffity of mixing the argumentative eloquence on occafions of perfuafion, the word *perfuafion* receives a double fignification ; for it is common to fay *perfuaded of a thing* as well as *perfuaded to it :* whereas the argumentative eloquence being fimple and uncompounded, the word *convince* cannot be applied to any, but its own peculiar purpofe of convincing the underftanding of the truth or falfhood of a pofition. It was therefore from its more comprehenfive ufe, and by way of abbreviation, that eloquence

quence was called by some great men, the SECT. *art of persuasion*, taking *persuasion* both in its II. proper and less proper sense *. And, had either CICERO or QUINTILIAN, put the art they taught in so ridiculous a light, as to deny, that it was likewise *the art of convincing by argument* †; we should, *ipso facto*, despise their

---

* Much of that fort of cunning nonsense, usually called wit, owes its being to the corruption and abuse of language. The double meaning of the word *persuadere* gave birth to that quaint expression recorded of St. AUGUSTIN, *Non persuadebis, etiamsi persuaseris*; which has no meaning at all, or only means, *Although you should convince me of the truth of what you advance, yet you shall never persuade me to take any step in consequence of such conviction.* The self same phrase is to be found in the *Plutus* of ARISTOPHANES; where one of the old men says to POVERTY, in answer to her harangue, ΟΥ ΓΑΡ ΠΕΙΣΕΙΣ ΟΥΔ' ΗΝ ΠΕΙΣΗΣ, and is explained as above by the Greek scholiast upon that passage.

† There cannot certainly be a more absurd attempt than that of persuading in matter of speculation without argument; and yet there are frequent phænomena that apologize, in some measure, for those who think it both practicable and easy. They may have perhaps observed the multitude persuaded of the truth of what the orator asserted, when there was nothing in his discourse that had the least appearance of argument; nay, when it was quite unintelligible.

This

PART their teſtimony, as coming from men whoſe
II. profeſſion was to deceive.

Of

This is, no doubt, a common fact; tho' it is not owing to any deluſive power of eloquence upon the imagination and paſſions, but acts by the bare force of perſonal credit and authority. The orator, by ſounding periods, learned terms, a pompous manner, an earneſt-neſs of geſture, and a look of ſincerity, convinces thoſe ſimpletons (for upon no other audience will ſuch oratory paſs) that he is a great, a learned, and an honeſt man; and then uſes this credit, ſo acquired, to faſten any opinion he pleaſes upon them. But this ridiculous ſort of prepoſſeſſion is not peculiarly the conſequence of eloquence; it will be found to follow alſo upon rank, riches, and many other advantages, where no ſuperiority of ſpeech or underſtanding is pretended: whatever is ſaid by a prince or a peer, carries with it great degree of perſuaſion from the rank of the perſon only. The ſame perſuaſion is generally attendant upon riches, *Et bene nummatum decorat ſuadela.* I lately heard a young gentleman relate an unlikely piece of news, in a company where it was received with ſome heſitation; upon which, he affirmed with great earneſtneſs, that it was certainly true, for he had heard it from a man of 4000*l.* a year. Handſome women have the ſame privilege of perſuading without argument, and by the like means; for, as their poet ſays,

> *Whatever they approve is ſweet,*
> *And all is ſenſe that they repeat.*

Fine

Of the argumentative eloquence we have Sect.
examples in the works of Isocrates, II.
Lucian, and other orators; who have had
queſtions in philoſophy, law, ſpeculative
politics, or philology for their topics. Of
the mixed kind we find numberleſs examples in the hiſtorians, and in the orations of
thoſe who have engaged in pleading cauſes,
or in the practice of war, divinity, or politics.
Amongſt the moſt famous in that way are
Demosthenes and Cicero; of whom,
Demosthenes apply'd himſelf chiefly, if
not altogether, to the underſtanding of his
auditors; even in thoſe orations, his *Philip-*
pics, where he meant to animate and rouſe
them

Fine cloaths, a decent gown and band, a diamond
ring, are all inſtruments of great energy in promoting
this ſort of conviction. Nay, there are aſſemblies, tho'
I believe, only of the fanatical ſort, where the reverſe
of all thoſe; to wit, the orator's bad language, auk-
ward delivery, poverty, mean condition, and unfaſhion-
able apparel, will give him great credit in the *eyes* of
his *hearers*, and produce conviction out of falſhood and
abſurdity. So that this perſuaſion, when it is produced,
is not ſo much a proof of the power of eloquence, as
of the weakneſs of underſtanding in the generality of
men; who have ſeldom any opinions, but what are ob-
truded upon them by authority.

PART them to action; whilst CICERO, adapting
I. himself to the times in which he lived, often
throws in a greater share of the pathetic
than would have succeeded with a people in
whom the reasoning faculty was more cultivated. This is the cause, as the Essay writer
observes, *that severe and able judges have prefer'd* DEMOSTHENES *to* CICERO; *for, as the
imagination and passions are then most refined
and just, when they bear to the same point
with reason; so that species of eloquence is the
noblest, which tends to conduct them thither* *.

In my next section I shall endeavour to
show, in what manner Ridicule becomes a
branch of this *noblest species of eloquence*; and
cannot conceive, upon what grounds my
Lord SHAFTSBURY's antagonist gave it a place
amongst the pathetic, or those which act by
an application to the passions. He says it
excites

* It is remarkable, that the words used to express the
eloquence of Greece and Rome, convey a just idea of
their several characters. In Greek, a piece of eloquence, let the subject be what it will, is called *logos*,
a *discourse*; and the person who delivers it, *rhetor*,
or *speaker*; whereas, in Latin, the performance is
called *oratio*, from *orare* to entreat, plead, or beg;
and the performer is called *orator*, an entreater, pleader,
or beggar.

excites the paſſion of contempt. Allowing Sᴇᴄᴛ.
him that contempt and laughter (the latter II.
of which Ridicule never fails to excite) are
both of them paſſions; a very little reflection will convince us, that Ridicule is not
therefore to be ranked amongſt the pathetic
kinds of eloquence; becauſe, in pathetic
eloquence, the paſſions are the inſtruments,
upon which the artiſt plays, in order to produce that perſuaſion he aims at: whereas,
contempt and laughter, call them what you
will, are, in matters of enquiry, the conſequences of the detection of that ſort of
falſhood, which we call the ridiculous; and
are not the means, but the end †.

† Some people may imagine, becauſe pathetic is
derived from *pathos* paſſion, that therefore every thing,
wherein paſſion is concerned, either as cauſe, means
or conſequence, muſt be pathetic. At this rate a ſlap
in the face would be pathetic; if either he who received,
or he who gave it happened to be in a paſſion. But
this is truſting too much to the infallibility of ſyllables.

SECT.

SECTION III.

PART
I.

WHEN a general marches his army into the enemy's country, he never thinks it confiftent with prudence to leave any fortified place behind him untaken, unlefs the garrifon is very contemptible. In like manner, he who ftrives upon paper to extend the dominions of truth, fhould take care to obviate all the objections that have been offered againft the caufe he under-takes, however groundlefs they may appear to him, while they are fo plaufible as to have the countenance of fome men of fenfe. It is for this reafon, that a fection of this fhort work has been wholly employed in adjufting certain differences betwixt elo-quence and argument, fuggefted by the author of the effays; a tafk, which would not otherwife have been neceffary: fince whatever is employed in the fearch of truth, whether it be addreffed to men's knowledge or their prejudices, whether it tends to con-duct or miflead, muft ever be addreffed to the underftanding; and, if eloquence, of

that

that sort of eloquence which consists of SECT. argument alone. III.

Having thus satisfied myself, and perhaps some of my readers, of one important truth, *that argumentative Ridicule is argumentative*, and consequently one of the methods of reasoning: I will venture a step farther, and assert, that it is one of the methods the best founded, the easiest comprehended, and the least subject to fallacy; for it will always be found, AN APPEAL TO EXPERIENCE *by some familiar image or allusion, which convinces by the justness, while it pleases by the novelty and contrast of its application.*

It is in this last quality, *novelty*, that distinguishes it from what is commonly called serious reasoning; and it is the first, *justness*, that distinguishes it from buffoonery or false Ridicule: for *false Ridicule is an appeal to false facts, or to true facts not parallel or applicable to the point in question.* Its name of Ridicule it receives only from a consequence, that never fails to attend it; for a serious falshood is never confuted by a sudden allusion to a trivial or domestic fact,

C without

without raiſing a ſmile or laugh in the
hearers.

Thoſe who are not willing to receive theſe
properties of Ridicule upon my bare aſſertion, muſt look for the proof of them in
the works of thoſe authors, who have been
moſt famous for their excellency in that way
of writing. There it was that theſe aſſer-
tions were formed, and thither I refer my
reader; not imagining that he would reſt the
cauſe upon any inſtances, which I might
partially chuſe in its ſupport. However,
by way of illuſtration at leaſt, I will give
one inſtance of true, and another of falſe
Ridicule; which I have choſen out of a
great number, becauſe they both belong to
one tranſaction, and that of a nature very
public and intereſting.

When that famous bill, in the year 1733,
called the Exciſe Scheme, was upon the
point of being carried in the Houſe of
Commons, a number of the moſt ſub-
ſtantial merchants of the city of London,
agreed to ſign a petition againſt it; and,
that it might come with what they called
greater weight, they proceeded in a long
                                    train

train of coaches and chariots to prefent it themfelves in a body. This petition, and the formidable cavalcade that attended it, were no fooner made known to the houfe than the chief minifter ftood up and fpoke againft the manner of prefenting it with great eloquence and fpirit; faying, amongft other things, That, altho' thofe gentlemen were contented in their writing with the title of humble petitioners, their appearance in Palace-Yard gave them more the air of another fort of petitioners, commonly known by the name of *Sturdy Beggars*. An image that gives a jufter idea of the illegallity and impropriety of their proceeding, than a regular oration of half an hour could have effected. For what ought to give weight to a petition in an affair of that importance to the nation, but the matter and reafons of the petition itfelf? And what could be more juft than to call thofe *Sturdy Beggars*, who, under pretence of petitioning, meant to extort what they wanted, by intimidating the members of parliament, and bullying the legiflature?

How then was this to be anfwered? It is, I muft own, a puzzling queftion. And

yet

PART yet an anfwer, of fome fort or other, was
I.   abfolutely neceffary, to prevent the party
from being delivered over to eternal laughter
and confufion of face. For, as POPE fays,

> *To vice and folly to confine the jeft,*
> *Sets half the world, God knows, againft the*
>   *reft ;*
> *Did not the fneer of more impartial men*
> *At fenfe and virtue ballance all again :*
> *Judicious wits fpread wide the ridicule,*
> *And charitably comfort knave and fool.*

With this humane defign, one of the
ringleaders of the patriots, for the time
being, rofe up; and, without taking notice
of the intention of the minifter's fpeech,
which was expreffed in a manner not at all
ambiguous, laid hold, with great feeming
heat, of the word *Beggar* ; wondring to
hear any man call thofe *Beggars,* who were
the pillars of the national commerce, and
who had perfonally fo great a fhare of the
national property; enlarging much upon
their riches, which had never been brought
into queftion; and fiinifhing the harangue
with a hiftory of the mifchiefs that befel the
government of Flanders, by a governor
                              contemptuoufly

contemptuously beſtowing the appellation of *Gueux* upon the citizens of Ghent. See all on a ſudden the tables turned. For this rea-ſoning, ſuch as it was, favoured the deſigns of the party, and the then reigning preju-dices of the vulgar; and, in conſequence of it, a ballad was compoſed, beginning

> *Of all the trades of London*
>   *A beggar's trade's the beſt,*
> *Since* BOB *allows us that trade*
>   *Who ruins all the reſt* ;
>   *And a begging we muſt go.*

Which acknowledged the merchants to be *beggars*, and put their beggary in a mul-titude of new and diverting lights, not very honourable for the man who had obtained, for many years, the ſole adminiſtration of public affairs ; and who had ſo inſolently, as was ſuppoſed, upbraided them with that miſery, of which he muſt have been the principal cauſe.

This, in a week's time, was ſpread over the moſt diſtant parts of the iſland, and raiſed an enthuſiaſtic rage in the populace,

C 3   that

PART that might have been attended with the moſt
I. cruel conſequences, if any accident had put
it in motion. For, as true Ridicule is one
of the moſt forcible and expeditious of all
the methods of reaſoning; ſo falſe Ridicule,
whenever it can be brought to take effect, as
it is the quickeſt, is the moſt to be dreaded
of all the methods of ſophiſtry.

Had the chief miniſter really called the
merchants of London *Beggars,* he would
have furniſhed evidence, from his own
mouth, for putting his adminiſtration in the
moſt contemptible light; and the *ballad* would
have been true Ridicule: but, as that pretended fact was known, to the ſober and
well informed to be falſe, the performance
could not to any ſuch appear otherwiſe, than
as a ſophiſtical piece of buffoonery.

S E C T.

SECT. IV.

IT will probably be objected to Ridicule, that, even as it has been describ'd and examplify'd in the foregoing Section, it is capable of serving the purpose of screening imposture, as well as of exposing it ; and therefore a very ambiguous and insufficient *criterion* of truth. This objection is not without foundation. But if we nicely examine the several instances of false Ridicule from whence it arises, the objection will be found not owing to any imperfection in the nature of Ridicule, but to the weakness and prejudice of those for whose conviction it is intended. He who should find out a method, by the immediate application of which fools and prejudiced persons might be enabled to distinguish truth from falshood, would find a philosopher's stone indeed. But there is no likelihood that such a *succedaneum* for good sense will ever be found, or that it was ever intended by the Almighty, who is equally the father of the wise and of the silly ; and who has, no doubt, ordained all those diversities, which exist in nature, for the

happi-

PART happiness of the whole. It is he who has
 I. given, according to the poet,

Fear to the statesman, rashness to the chief,
To kings presumption, and to crouds belief.

Mundus vult decipi : and I write not for the
many, whom it would be perhaps as unfit, as it is impossible to undeceive. What
species of reasoning is there, the most serious and formal, that has not been made the
channel for conveying error and absurdity to
the understanding, under the appearance of
truth? And when we say, that this sort of
reasoning is least liable to be abused, it is
saying as much for it, as can be said for most
things, in which the frail race of man is
concern'd. False reasoning, by the abuse of
words, is very easy and common, because
the ideas attached to general terms are very
various, indistinct, and easily confounded ;
but the properties of things, especially those
of a vulgar and domestic nature, in which
the force and pleasure of Ridicule chiefly
consists, cannot safely be summon'd for evidence to support any principle or general
assertion, unless that principle be true, and
consistent with the existence of things.

                                        But

But, however excellent this specific may SECT.
be, I will allow that, like other excellent IV.
remedies, it may become poison in the hands
of a quack; and that it is of consequence
to have an antidote always ready upon occasion. This we need not be long in search
of, since there is one handed down to us in
the works of a very ancient and eminent
physician, and which I am able to recommend upon my own repeated experience,
altho it has been discountenanced of late by
several apothecaries; either because they did
not understand the *recipe*, or because they
had not those drugs in their shops, that were
necessary for the composition.

To leave parables, and to explain myself
like a man of this world, this *recipe* is no
other than that rule of GORGIAS, quoted by
ARISTOTLE, which the critic upon the *Characteristicks* has re-translated and new-apply-
ed after my Lord SHAFTSBURY, and which
I shall take the like freedom of translating
again, and new-applying after him; always
however observing that good manners and
deference, which is due to a living author.

The

PART I.   The paſſage in ARISTOTLE tranſlated verbatim, runs thus, *But with regard to thoſe things that excite laughter, ſince they ſeem to have their uſe in debate, we ought*, ſays GORGIAS, *to diſcuſs the adverſary's ſerious argument by Ridicule, and his Ridicule by ſerious argument; rightly ſpeaking* *.

But, having expounded this paſſage with ſufficient accuracy, as far as regards the relation

---

* The original words are, ΠΕΡΙ ΔΕ ΤΩΝ ΓΕΛΟΙΩΝ, ΕΠΕΙΔΗ ΤΙΝΑ ΔΟΚΕΙ ΧΡΗΣΙΝ ΕΧΕΙΝ ΕΝ ΤΟΙΣ ΑΓΩΣΙ, ΚΑΙ ΔΕΙΝ, ΕΦΗ ΓΟΡΓΙΑΣ, ΤΗΝ ΜΕΝ ΣΠΟΥΔΗΝ ΔΙΑΦΘΕΙΡΕΙΝ ΤΩΝ ΕΝΑΝΤΙΩΝ, ΓΕΛΩΤΙ· ΤΟΝ ΔΕ ΓΕΛΩΤΑ, ΣΠΟΥΔΗ. ΟΡΘΩΣ ΛΕΓΩΝ. Rhet. lib. iii. cap. 18. And they are thus tranſlated by the author of the *Eſſays*. *As Ridicule ſeems to be of ſome uſe in pleading, it was the opinion of* GORGIAS *that you ought to confound your adverſary's ſerious argument by raillery, and his raillery by ſerious argument. And he judged well.* It were to be wiſhed that the tranſlator had inform'd us by what authority he has render'd the word ΔΙΑΦΘΕΙΡΕΙΝ *to confound*, in a diametrical oppoſition to all the hitherto known meanings of it. For what can be more oppoſite than *to confound* and *to ſeparate* ? ΔΙΑΦΘΕΙΡΕΙΝ in its moſt ſimple ſenſe, means *to ſeparate thoroughly*, and in all the uſual applications

lation betwixt Englifh and Greek words, my SECT.
work will be but half done, unlefs I tranflate IV.
thofe words again into their precife meaning,
and fhew what relation they have to realities.

All men, who engage in any controverfy
with the candid intention of difcovering truth,
cannot fail of obferving, how much their
laudable endeavours are obftructed by the
imperfection and abufe of language. I believe we may venture to fay, that this is the
very foul of controverfy, and that thinking
men could not difagree in their opinions
concerning any thing that comes within the
reach of human reafon, if it were poffible
to find a number of figns, that fhould, with
exactnefs, convey the fame ideas from one
perfon to another. Common language is
far from being equal to this purpofe; and
the only remedy for the defect is, by definitions and examples to explain the principal terms that are to be employed; and then

plications very little deviates from this its original meaning. Such are to *demolifh, confume, corrupt, difcufs*. Of
thefe I have made ufe of the laft, as it has the additional authority and fupport of all the Latin tranfla-
tors of this paffage, that have fallen into my hands.

it

PART it fignifies little, what thefe terms are; whe-
  I.   ther they are fuch as have been already ufed,
or others arbitrarily devifed for the occafion.

The term *Ridicule* has been already defin'd and examplify'd; fo that there can be
no difficulty, at leaft with regard to my idea
of it; but the term *ferious argument* bears
fo many different meanings, that to ufe it
without the like caution would be to involve
us in a labyrinth of confufion. However,
before I pretend to define its proper meaning in the above fentence in ARISTOTLE, I
will firft point out, in a few lines, how this
definition comes to be neceffary; and the
rather, as the enquiry is not barely verbal,
but will likewife throw fome light upon the
main fubject.

There is, and no doubt always has been,
in all places, in ancient Athens, as well as
in modern London, a great number of fhal-
low-pated people, who feeing the tribute of
applaufe, and kind reception, that never fails
to be paid to true wit and humour, are
willing to have likewife their fhare of it;
but, not being bleft with the lawful means,

viz.

viz. a lively fancy, and a found judgment,
employ fuch means as nature has beftowed
upon them. Some of thefe facetious gentlemen will lay joint-ftools in the way of their
companions, pin their fkirts to the table-
cloth, archly flip away their chairs from under them, and abundance of other conceits,
from whence nothing but a monkey could
claim any merit. But thofe fhin-breaking,
clothes-daubing, chair-withdrawing wits, are
each of them a CERVANTES or a CHESTER-
FIELD, in comparifon of another fort of
idiotical vermin, who to be thought witty,
will deceive you by a direct lie; or keep you
a confiderable time in fufpenfe by an ambiguity; and then laugh, and tell you *it was
a joke.* The confequences of this pitiful
practice are deplorable; for, by its frequency,
not only the language is corrupted by the
mifapplication of words; but that innocence,
confidence, and fecurity, which conftitute the
great pleafure and dignity of converfation,
amongft thofe of liberal minds, is often hurt
and confounded. How often do we hear
even men of tolerable breeding, afk one another, *Are you in jeft or ferious?* that is, *Do
you lie or fpeak truth?* and yet by the common-
nefs

ness of this sort of jesting not incur the re-sentment, that would follow the question properly expressed.

We see therefore, that by *serious* is often meant *sincere* and *in earnest* ; and by jesting, their opposites, *lying* and *trifling* ; but in this treatise we allow no such meaning to them ; and I trust that in this we walk hand in hand with ARISTOTLE. Ridicule, or true jesting, is, with regard to sincerity, as much serious, as any other method of reasoning ; and the more apt to promote both its desired consequences of conviction and laughter, the more the sentiment of the dispenser is sincere, and his deportment grave. What then is it which distinguishes, what we call *serious argument* from *Ridicule ?* That will be easily found, if the reader will give himself the trouble of turning back to that place, where I account for the name of *Ridicule* ; he will there find, that it is so called *from its exciting laughter in the hearers* ; so, in like manner, the other sorts of reasoning are called *serious*, from their *not exciting laughter*, without any regard to their being sincere or otherwise.

Having

Having thus fully explained my terms, I will proceed to illuftrate the rule of GOR- GIAS, by fhewing *that a jeft, that will not bear a ferious examination, is certainly falfe wit* ; and likewife, however *hardy* it may appear to the critic upon Lord SHAFTSBURY, *that an argument, that will not bear Ridicule, is certainly falfe logic.* In other words, *that gravity is the proper teft of Ridicule, and Ridicule the proper teft of gravity*; even as the rule of addition is the teft of fubtraction, and fubtraction of addition. I hope that gentleman will not call this likewife, *a fee-faw fort of proof,* and fay, it is *trying the juftnefs of the fquare by the work that is formed by it* *.

But one fhort ftory will clear up this matter better than a volume of dry terms ; and one now occurs to my memory, which, I believe, I have formerly met with in the Cambridge jefts, or fome other valuable repofitory of that kind.

* *Effay on the Characterifticks*, Sect. IX.

A3

PART
I.
As an Oxford ſcholar was ſitting at ſupper, in the Chriſtmaſs vacation, with his father and mother, plain ſenſible country-people, the diſcourſe fell, as is natural, upon the univerſity ; and led the youth inſenſibly into a declamation in praiſe of learning in general, and particularly of logic. I ſhould be glad to know, ſays the father, what this ſame logic is, you are ſo mightily fond of. It is, ſays the ſcholar, the art of making people believe whatever we pleaſe. Ay, ſays the old man, that's curious indeed. Prithee, Tom, give your mother and me a ſhort flouriſh of it, that we may have ſome reaſon to admire as well as you. Juſt as he ſpoke, a couple of minc'd pyes being ſet upon the table ; I will prove, ſays the ſcholar, that here are three pyes. That will oblige us extremely, ſays the old folks. Nothing more eaſy, ſays the ſon. You will grant me, that this is one. Yes. And that this is two. No doubt. Why then, ſays this young Plato, if you put one and two together, they make three. O wonderful ! cries the farmer. Then, my dear, continues he, addreſſing himſelf to his wife, you

ſhall

ſhall take one pye, I another, and Tom ſhall SECT.
have the third, to encourage him in the pur- IV.
ſuit of ſuch excellent ſtudies.

Here is an example of *ſerious argument*
without truth in itſelf, or ſincerity in the perſon by whom it is uſed ; and here is *Ridicule*
to demoliſh it, which is true, and in earneſt.
If any one objects to my example, that what
I call *ſerious* argument is in reality ridiculous
and ſilly ; it is fit, that I inform ſuch an ob-
jector, once for all, that it is only ſuch ſerious argument, that Ridicule pretends to
deſtroy ; and that it is only ſuch ſerious argument, that ſhuns and diſclaims the teſt of
Ridicule. Had our ſcholar contented himſelf with proving, that two pyes and one
made three, he might have ſet all the Ridicule of RABELAIS at defiance. So much
for logic, now for Ridicule.

This diverting manner of reaſoning, altho the leaſt fitted, as has been before obſerved, to convince people of what is contrary to the nature of things ; has been ne-
vertheleſs ſometimes employed for that purpoſe, and perhaps not without ſome ſucceſs,

D   upon

upon minds weak and prejudiced: and being of a rapid and collective nature, it is
neceſſary to ſtop its progreſs by ſome method of reaſoning more ſlow and analytical;
which may, like FABIUS againſt HANNI-
BAL, *cunctando reſtituere rem.*

Dr. SWIFT, whoſe works afford many
examples of *true Ridicule,* now and then
gives us an inſtance of the *falſe,* chiefly, if
not altogether, owing to the force of party-
ſpirit; which never fails to incline thoſe,
who are under its influence, to a perverſion
of truth, let their good ſenſe and natural
love of truth be ever ſo great. It was this
ſpirit which prompted that ingenious writer,
born with a diſpoſition the moſt remote from
ſlaviſh, to endeavour to ridicule the whig
principle of *the right in the people of re-
ſiſting tyrants;* a principle which is in reality
the ſentiment of human nature, and which
by an appeal to numberleſs facts throws the
Ridicule with irreſiſtible force upon its oppoſers. What then could thoſe expect, who
were ſo raſh as to engage common ſenſe at
her own weapons, but to leave a ſad example
of the inſufficiency of human wit, when
improperly and unworthily applied?

This

This waggery has for title, *Mrs.* BULL's *vindication of the indefeasible right of Cuckoldom incumbent upon wives, in case of the tyranny, infidelity, or insufficiency of their husband's; being a full answer to the Doctor's sermon against Adultery.* And it is introduced into that excellent piece of allegorical humour, *The History of John Bull*, of which it makes a part; as a wen makes a part of the fair body that is disgraced by it.

To detect the fallacy of this pretended piece of Ridicule, let us follow the advice of ARISTOTLE, and reduce it to the formality of a syllogism or two. As thus : First, the author ironically informs you, that

A wife is to her husband, what a nation is to its king :

Now, it being lawful for a nation to shake off its king whenever it is displeased with him, and to take another in his room :

Ergo, it is lawful for a wife to renounce her husband, whenever he incurs her displeasure, and to confer her favours upon any one she likes better.

D 2

To

PART I.

To make this ironical fyllogifm ferve the purpofe of the party, the faithful reader is charitably fuppofed to refolve it into the following; which he will not fail to do, *coute qui'l coute*, if he be a true fon of SACHEVE-REL.

It is contrary to all order and the common fenfe of mankind, that a wife fhould, upon any occafion, think herfelf authorifed to abjure her fidelity to her hufband.

And a nation being exactly to its king, what a wife is to her hufband:

Ergo, it is contrary to common fenfe to believe, that any failure in a king can ever abfolve his fubjects from their allegiance. *Quod erat demonftrandum.*

It requires very little fcrutiny to difcover, wherein the fallacy lies of this reafoning; for it appears, at the firft glance, that the whole is founded upon a fuppofition, that a king ftands in the fame relation to the people he governs, that a hufband does to his wife: which is fo manifeftly otherwife, that it were an abufe of paper to fhew in how many points the difference confifts.

Befides,

Besides, the author, for the sake of this absurd buffoonery, has destroyed that allegorical
consistency which is so divertingly preserved
throughout the rest of the performance. And
whereas Mr. *Bull*, in the body of the work,
represents the English nation, and Mrs. *Bull*
the parliament; in this excrescence Mr.
Bull is forced to represent the king of England, and Mrs. *Bull* the nation. An al-
gebraist, who, in the progress of his calcu-
lation, makes the letter *b* sometimes stand for
one number and sometimes for another, has
no chance of producing a solution, that will
do him credit. And, for my own part, if
I may be admitted an evidence, as well as
counsel, in this case, I declare, that I never
found, in reading these two chapters of
Swift, any more inclination to laugh, than
to be convinced; and therefore doubt not,
but the verdict will be brought in, *False Ridicule*, and consequently no test of truth.

SECTION V.

PART
I.

IT is not enough, that a pofition is falfe; to make it ridiculous, and a proper object for Ridicule, it muft likewife be Im-portant. When Horace fays, *Parturi-unt montes, nafcitur ridiculus mus,* he does not mean, that the moufe was ridiculous in itfelf; but that it only became fo by the mighty expectations, which this pompous and important delivery had occafioned. And although *importance* or *gravity* is not, as Lord Shaftsbury afferts, *the effence of im-pofture;* it is fo far the *effence* of the *ridiculous,* that it is eafy to produce a multitude of inftances, where Ridicule has juftly fallen upon fayings, that were not otherwife falfe, than as they were not adequate, nor of a piece, with the folemnity of the defign.

One of thefe examples is recorded of Diogenes the Cynic, which I fhall relate at length, for the benefit of fuch of my readers, as may not be particularly read in the hiftory of thofe *wags,* whom the ancients
called

called *philosophers*; and who, in reality, de- served that honoured name much better, than some of their more serious brethren, for reasons already hinted.

PLATO having defined a man *A two-legg'd animal without feathers*, in the hearing of DIOGENES, the defcription appeared to him extremely ridiculous, and he refolved to expose it to the laughter of the public. To do this effectually, he caft about in search of fome contemptible animal, that might answer the defcription; but could find none. Convinced at laft, that he could not attack his rival on the fide of *falshood*, he gave over that fearch; but, as he ftill lay open on the fide of *infignificance*, by a definition fo unbecoming the real dignity of the fubject, the fuppofed dignity of the philofopher, and the fcientific pomp of words in which it was dreffed; he refolved to make that example, which he ftrove in vain to find ready made. So having ftript a cock of its feathers, he hid it under his cloak, and fetting it fuddenly upon its legs, before PLATO and his ad-

D 4   mirers,

mirers, he cryed out, *Behold the man of* PLATO!

This was thought a witty thing, at the time, and has been handed down as such through many generations. It was certainly true Ridicule, as to *importance*; and yet the thing ridiculed was not shewn to be otherwise false, but the contrary; as the ridiculer was obliged to appeal, not to the nature of things, but to what was manifestly artificial.

But, to make Ridicule compleatly triumphant, it is necessary, that it should be employed upon what is compleatly ridiculous; that is, what is both *false* and *important*. It is for this reason, that of all the different absurdities, which have disgraced the human species, there is none, that has been the cause of so much true wit and Ridicule, as *false religion*. And indeed how is it possible for those, on whom the Almighty has bestowed faculties of mind superior to others, to employ them more properly than in vindicating his honour; and endeavouring to communicate their own just sentiments in a

familiar

familiar way to thofe of their fellow creatures, who are lefs happily endowed?

How neceffary a talk this has been, let all
hiftory teftify. For, from the moft early
times, there never has been wanting a fet of
impoftors, who made it their bufinefs to
practife upon the fear, ignorance, and credulity of the weaker and more numerous part
of mankind, by reprefenting the Eternal
Being not fuch as he appears in his glorious
works, but fuch as beft fuited their bafe
purpofes. And yet *in no time was God without witnefs*, as St. PAUL expreffes it; as
there have been found in every age fome
men of fuperior fenfe and honefty, who have
endeavoured, and often with fuccefs, to
withdraw their weak brethren from that
impious yoke, by expofing to laughter thofe
lies and abfurdities, which had been impofed
upon them inftead of fact and argument.

LUCIAN, one of the moft correct writers
amongft the ancients, and the greateft
mafter of that fort of analogical reafoning,
which we call Ridicule, has employed his
wit,

wit, with great fuccefs, againft the foolifh
worfhip and abominable notions of the
Deity, as by law and cuftom eftablifhed in
his days. And, before him many others,
particularly the Latin Satirifts, Juvenal,
Persius, and Horace, thought it their
duty to turn thofe ferious matters into merri-
ment. To eke out this fhort treatife, in the
German fafhion, with thread-bare fcraps of
Latin, and by quoting from authors, that
are intimately known to all thofe, who underftand the language in which they are written,
would be tirefome and impertinent. I will
therefore exemplify this part of my fubjeﬅ
by a piece of Ridicule, much more excellent, as well as more ancient, than any that
is to be found in the authors above mentioned, which is preferved in the latter part
of the 13th chapter of *The wifdom of* Solomon. I fhall infert the whole of it, that I
may be fure of indemnifying my reader for
his trouble, by prefenting him with a piece
of moft compleat *eloquence*, which might
not otherwife have fallen into his hands.

1. *Surely*

1. *Surely vain are all men by nature, who* SECT.
are ignorant of GOD, *and could not out of the* V.
good things that are seen, know him that is :
neither by considering the works, did they ac-
knowledge the work-mafter ;

2. *But deemed either fire, or wind, or the*
swift air, or the circle of the ftars, or the
violent water, or the lights of Heaven to be
the Gods which govern the world.

3. *With whofe beauty, if they being de-*
lighted, took them to be Gods; let them know
how much better the Lord of them is : for the
firft author of beauty hath created them.

4. *But if they were aftonifhed at their*
power and virtue, let them underftand by
them, how much mightier he is that made
them.

5. *For by the greatnefs and beauty of the*
creatures, proportionably the maker of them is
feen.

6. *But*

6. *But yet for this they are the less to be blamed : for they, peradventure, err seeking* God *and desirous to find him.*

7. *For, being conversant in his works, they search him diligently and believe their sight : because the things are beautiful that are seen.*

8. *Howbeit neither are they to be pardoned.*

9. *For if they were able to know so much, that they could aim at the world, how did they not sooner find out the* LORD *thereof?*

10. *But miserable are they, and in dead things is their hope, who called them gods which are the work of mens hands, gold and silver to shew art in, and resemblances of beasts, or a stone good for nothing, the work of an ancient hand.*

11. *Now a carpenter that felleth timber, after he hath sawn down a tree meet for the purpose, and taken off all the bark skilfully round*

round about, and hath wrought it handsomely,
and made a vessel thereof fit for the service of
man's life *.

12. *And, after spending the refuse of his
work to dress his meat, hath filled himself*;

13. *And taking the very refuse among those
which served to no use, (being a crooked
piece of wood and full of knots) hath carv-
ed it diligently when he had nothing else to
do, and formed it by the skill of his understanding, and fashioned it to the image of
a man*;

14. *Or made it like some vile beast, laying it over with vermilion, and with paint*

---

* The kindred, which, in a carver's shop, a bench or
stool may claim to a god, is no less obvious to the
sensible few, than it is comical. We find it accordingly introduced by HORACE, who strikes at the whole
pandæmonium of heathen idolatry, through the sides of
their brother PRIAPUS,

> *Olim truncus eram ficulnus, inutile lignum :*
> *Cum faber incertus scamnum faceretne Priapum,*
> *Maluit esse Deum.*   L. 1. Sat. 8.

3   *colouring*

colouring it red, and covering every spot there-in.

15. *And when he had made a convenient room for it, set it in a wall, and made it fast with iron :*

16. *For he provided for it that it might not fall, knowing that it was unable to help itself, (for it is an image and hath need of help.)*

17. *Then maketh he prayer for his goods, for his wife and children, and is not ashamed to speak to that which hath no life.*

18. *For health, he calleth upon that which is weak: for life, prayeth to that which is dead: for aid, humbly beseecheth that which hath least means to help: and, for a good journey, he asketh of that which cannot set a foot forward :*

19. *And for gaining and getting, and for good success of his hands, asketh ability to do, of him that is most unable to do any thing.*

Here

Here is truly *serious reasoning*, that tends
by investigation to the knowledge of the Divine Being, as far as human faculties are capable to go, and which Momus himself would
not be able to ridicule ; and here is *Ridicule*
to expose the absurdity of the popular notions and practices, that will stand the examination of ARISTOTLE with all his dialectics.

The Critic upon Lord SHAFTSBURY appears however to be a great enemy to this
familiar way of trying religious opinions ;
and finishes the 7th section of his *Essay* with
what he seems to think very much to its dif-
advantage, and the disadvantage of Ridicule
in general, in these words : *It seems therefore,
that his Lordship's observation (which contains
the quintessence of his associate's work, and
which probably was the leaven, that leavened
the whole lump of malice and dulness) instead
of being favourable to Ridicule, as a test of
truth, can only tend to disgrace it. For since
every religious and unbelieving sect have alike*
SUCCESSFULLY EMPLOYED IT IN SUPPORT-
ING *their respective tenets, and in rendering
those of their adversaries contemptible ; it
follows, inasmuch as doctrines, which are*
essentially

essentially repugnant, cannot all be true; that Ridicule is one of the most powerful engines, by which error can be maintained and established †.

This is strong, pointed, and seems to conclude the argument as thoroughly as it concludes the section. What a pity it is, that it should have no better foundation than what the author himself owns to be in the former sentence, *a leavened lump of malice and dulness.*

† The observation of Lord SHAFTSBURY here alluded to, is to be found in his foregoing leaf, when speaking of modern zealots, he tells us, that *Whatever they think grave and solemn, they suppose must never be treated out of a grave and solemn way; though what another thinks so, they can be contented to treat otherwise, and are fond to try the test of Ridicule against any opinion besides their own.* But how the remarker should find in these words any thing concerning the *support* of different opinions, by the means of Ridicule, it is difficult to guess. He likewise accuses Mr. COLLINS, whom he calls *his associate*, of this gross absurdity; and perhaps he may be guilty of it. But as he has not quoted any passage, or so much as mentioned the name of the work where it is to be found; we have reason to doubt, whether he has not mistaken Mr. COLLINS, as much as he has my Lord SHAFTSBURY. But supposing Lord SHAFTSBURY and his associates to be as dull and malicious, as he has been pleased to represent them, what is it to the merits of Ridicule?

It

It is certainly true, that many religious Sect.
sects have successfully employed Ridicule, V.
in *rendering the tenets of their adversaries con-*
temptible; but how is it possible that an in-
strument, whose professed use is to pull down,
should be employed in *supporting* any sect of
religion, except there were only two sects of
religion in the world, and one of them necessarily true; whereas it is possible there
may be five hundred, and all, but one, false
and ridiculous. Was there ever any author
so weak as to fancy, that where two men of
war are pelting one another, either of them
proposes to mend his own rigging by the
shot, which he pours into his adversary? Is
the worship of Venus or Ganymede at all
more established by the excellent jokes, which
Juvenal has thrown at the crocodile and
onion gods of the Egyptians? Or suppose a
Catholic should raise the laugh ever so properly against the worship of Fum Ho, and
the Chinese should return it full upon St.
Anthony of Padua; would any one be
more convinced of the truth of the Chinese
or Popish idolatry, than he was before? Did
Pascal's admired Ridicule of the Jesuits
prove any thing towards the truth of Janse-

E   nism?

PART nifm? No. After all his wit, their doctrines
I. of the *grace of congruity*, and *grace of efficacy*, continue to be equally unintelligible, and equally as ufelefs as ever: and both fides were expofed to the Ridicule of more unpaffionate minds; by whofe means, as VOLTAIRE obferves, France was eafed of a difpute that equally difgraced chriftianity, learning, and the human underftanding*.

Indeed when two fects, in the fame country, while they appear to be contending for the truth of their feveral opinions, are in reality contending for power and riches; that fect, which deftroys its adverfary by any means, direct or finifter, by ferioufnefs, ridicule, or blows, eftablifhes itfelf as effectually as it defires; and huzzas, like a victorious fhip, that has funk its enemy; tho',

---

* *On fe fouvient, avec quel mepris le duc d' Orleans et fon miniftre parlaient des querelles qu'ils appaifcrent; quel ridicule ils jetterent fur cette guerre de controverfe. Ce mepris et ce ridicule ne fervirent pas peu a la paix. On fe laffe enfin de combattre, pour des querelles dont le monde rit.*

Siecle de Louis 14. *chap.* du Janfenifme.

with

w th twenty fhots in its own hull, half its
men flain, and not a maft ftanding.

It is much to the honour of the prefent
ftate of this country, that, notwithftanding
the univerfal toleration, the liberty of the
prefs, and the fecurity with which all opinions may be canvaffed, there is little or nothing offered tending to ridicule the religion,
that is either by law eftablifhed or tolerated.
It has not been fo always, and, I believe,
it will be found, that the books and papers
of Ridicule upon religious fubjects, have been
much more numerous at any time, between the
reformation and the acceffion of his prefent
majefty; than they have been during his happy
reign. And the reafon feems to be obvious.
For, in former reigns, the factions which
tore the bowels of the nation, were formed
of certain religious fects, who carried creeds
for their banners, differing often in the meereft
trifles; which trifles however being the
bond of union of each party, as well as the
pretended caufe of divifion, were magnified
into matters of the greateft IMPORTANCE by
their feveral leaders and trumpeters; fo that

E 2   they

PART I.

they became from contemptible excrescences to be the whole, almost, of the religion of the times.

In this every way polemical state of our unhappy country, when the spirit of controversy descended so low, as to excite little misses of ten years old, to pull caps about *the divine right of episcopacy*, or *the validity of lay baptism*; when it rose so high, as to make one of the greatest epic poets that any age has furnished, introduce the Almighty discoursing like a school-divine *, and the devils amusing themselves in hell with metaphysical cunnundrums †; when the friends of peace and liberty were by turns terrified with the prospect of anarchy, from the hair-brained enthusiasm of the sectaries; and of popish tyranny, under a bigotted king. Then it was, that BUTLER, TINDAL, TRENCHARD, GORDON, and many others rose up

---

* MILTON's *Paradise-Lost*, Book III.

† *Others apart sat on a hill retir'd*
   In thoughts more elevate, and reason'd high
   Of providence, foreknowledge, will, and fate;
   Fixt fate, free will, foreknowledge absolute;
   And found no end, in wand'ring mazes lost.

Book II.

to

to reap this fat harvest, which the heats of SECT.
the times had brought to maturity; then it V.
was, that Dr. SWIFT wrote his *Tale of a*
Tub, to aid the serious pen of Archbishop
TILLOTSON and other learned and good men,
whose manner of writing was not so calculated to produce the contempt which they
aimed at, and which the safety and happiness of our church and state required *.

But of late years the persons, who have
had the administration of public affairs, have
found, that government can be maintained
with more security by other means, than by
making

* Lord ORRERY has summed up the excellency of
the Tale of the Tub in the following words : *Throughout
the whole piece there is a vein of Ridicule and good humour,
that laughs pedantry and affectation into the lowest degree
of contempt*; *and exposes the character of* JACK *and*
PETER, *in such a manner as never will be forgiven, and
never can be answered.*

           Remarks on Dr. SWIFT, Lett. xxiii.

It does however more than barely laugh at pedantry and affectation, which is properly the office of
that sort of Ridicule, whose object is manner and action ;
and of which I shall treat in the second part of this
essay. *The Tale of the Tub*, like *Don Quixote*, is of the
argumentive kind of Ridicule, whose business is to oppose
false opinions ; and operates by raising up fictitious characters

PART making a ſtalking-horſe of religion ; ſo that
I. thoſe trifling diſtinctions, invented and kept
up to enflame the populace on either ſide,
loſing their intended effect, loſt by degrees
their IMPORTANCE, and by ceaſing to be
important, have ceaſed to be the objects of
Ridicule. Religion is now become in England, almoſt † what it was at firſt intended to
be ; not a tool for the politic and the ſeditious
to work withal, but a matter entirely of
private

racters to act in familiar occurrences in life, upon principles falſe and chimerical, and by repreſenting the
obvious conſequences of ſuch a proceeding, convincing
the reader of the falſhood and abſurdity of ſuch principles and opinions. This is called, in common language,
with great propriety, *putting thoſe opinions to the proof*;
and is, of all the modes of Ridicule that ever were
found out, the faireſt as well as the moſt diverting.

† The word *almoſt*, although unmuſical in the
ſentence, cannot, with a ſafe conſcience, be left out ;
becauſe we can never be ſaid to be *altogether* in that ſtate
of liberty and common ſenſe, to which the conſtitution
of this kingdom has been verging for this hundred years
paſt, while there is any law in force to puniſh thoſe, who
differ in opinion from their rulers in matters merely
ſpeculative. Perhaps there are people, who will be
ſurpriſed when they hear the word *puniſhment*, fancying
that it has no other meaning than to burn, fine and
impriſon. But their ſurpriſe will perhaps ceaſe,
when

private concern, fubject to no jurifdiction, Sect.
but that of confcience or private opinion; V.
which will ever be moft refpectable when moft
divefted of worldly power and riches; and
will ever moft deferve the approbation of the
wife and virtuous, the lefs noife it makes.

when they are put in mind, that to declare a man incapable of holding any place of truft or profit under the
government, is often decreed in court as a punifhment
for very great offences: and, whilft a law fubfifts to
inflict fuch a ftigma upon ufeful fubjects, who diffent
from the parliamentary creed, the toleration is far from
being compleat.

SECT. VI.

PATT
I.

BESIDES philofophical truth, which is required in pofitions that are pre-fented immediately to the underftanding, there is a thing called POETICAL TRUTH, which is required in thofe images, which are prefented to the fancy, either to beautify or illuftrate compofitions in poetry, of which they may be called the effence. Thefe pafs commonly by the name of *allegories*, *meta-phors* or *fimilies*; and are always to be con-demned as falfe, whenever they prefent any idea to the imagination that is abfurd, mean, or unfuitable.

To men of a lively and orderly fancy, to whom every word produces the idea, of which it is a fign, with diftinctnefs and precifion, every incongruity of that fort is immediately manifeft; but, to thofe who are not bleft with this faculty, which is often called *tafte*, in fo eminent a degree, fome foreign help is neceffary, in order to furnifh their judgment with more perfect materials to exercife itfelf upon. And, of all the methods fuggefted

by

by critics for this purpose, there is none
quicker or surer, than one recommend in
the *Spectator*, N°. 595, and that is, to
call in the assistance of the pencil, and try
what effect such metaphors or imagery would
have, when exhibited upon canvass. This
is nothing but that APPEAL FROM WORDS
TO FACTS of which I have been hitherto
treating; and which will be a constant de-
tector of the false and ridiculous, whenever
it obtrudes itself.

Suppose, for instance, the friends of the
church of England should have a desire to
expose the wild and absurd expressions, used
by the growing sect of Moravians in their
public worship. In what manner is this
most effectually to be done?

According to my Lord SHAFTSBURY's
system of Ridicule, PUNCH would be employed to sing a hymn out of their *Salt-book*
in broken English, accompanied with a
thorough bass upon the *Salt-box*, instead of
an organ; and, to render it more savoury, to
change the words here and there into others,
for which his oratory is chiefly admired,

While

PART
I.
While this was performing, the mob of Smithfield, and, perhaps, politer people would laugh; but it would be at PUNCH for his naftinefs and monky-tricks, while the brethren would efcape unhurt.

This is not Ridicule, but only burlefque and waggery. But if any man has a mind to raife an effectual laugh at thefe devout pro-ceedings, let him open the book at page 53, and with a compofed countenance, and a tone of voice fit for the leffon of the day, read aloud:

> *Lovely fide-hole take in me,*
> *Let me ever be in thee;*
> *O fide-hole's wound, my heart and foul*
> *Does pant for thy fo lovely hole.*
> *Lovely fide-hole take in me,*
> *Let me ever be in thee:*
> *If I once fecurely fit,*
> *In the lovely fide-hole's fplit,*
> *O then I for ever dwell*
> *In the lovely* PLEURA's *cell :*
> *O then I,* &c.

OR,

OR,

*Ye children, where do you dwell, where is
    your ground,
Where is the beft care for fuch little ones found?
We dwell in the wound-holes, in* JESU'S *flefh
    made,
The holy church cares for, and lends us her aid.*

*But will for fuch number of doves room be
    found,
In the narrow fpace of the holy fide's wound?
O yes, and befides there is room for to fit,
In all the holes of the lamb's hands and feet.*

*What is it that in all your meetings refounds?
One fpeaks, hears, and fings here at all times
    of wounds;
One fpeaks, hears, and fings here at all times
    of wounds;
Wounds, wounds, again wound-holes, and no-
    thing but wounds :* &c. &c. &c.

This is burlefque enough of itfelf, and
would alone be fufficient to raife laughter in
every one, who felt the proper force of the
         words;

words; but it is as certain, at the same time, that there are thousands, in whom they raise rapture and enthusiasm. From whence can this strange effect, upon a particular set of people, proceed? I make no doubt, but that it is caused by long and early habitude, which has destroyed or changed the ideas in their minds, upon this occasion, which those words naturally excite at other times, producing no image, but what is confused, indistinct, and no doubt very different in one of the society, from what it does in another. But let any engraver adorn their hymn book with a few cuts, let him draw men, women and children creeping into the side-hole, and nestling in it like wasps in a hollow tree; and there is great reason to believe, that there are none of the faithful, however damaged in their understanding, but would see the absurdity and nastiness of this their allegory; and would either laugh or be angry, according as pride happened to be more or less predominant in their several constitutions.

It

It is not the performance alone of those High German artifts, that ought to be examined by this rule; it is a certain teft for the foundnefs of every piece of poetry whatfoever; but a teft fo fevere, that the beft of them all will fometimes fhrink at it. There are many defcriptions in the great MILTON, which pafs very currently in blank verfe, and yet would make but a poor or difgufting appearance in colours, and fome of them entirely incapable of delineation.

Perhaps HOMER himfelf may not be, upon every occafion, exempt from this charge. His defcription of NEPTUNE's progrefs from Somothrace to Æge (240 miles) in four ftrides *, has been much admired by fome critics

---

* ΤΡΙΣ ΜΕΝ ΟΡΕΞΑΤ' ΙΩΝ, ΤΟ ΔΕ ΤΕΤΡΑΤΟΝ
    ΙΚΕΤΟ ΤΕΚΜΩΡ
    ΑΙΓΑΣ.   Iliad, 12.

From realm to realm three ample ftrides he took,
And at the fourth the diftant Æge fhook.   POPE.

Madam DACIER has omitted this in her tranflation; for which Mr. POPE condemns her; not for want of fidelity, but want of tafte, in paffing over a ftroke of poetry

PART critics for its sublimity; but it is certainly not
I.   in the power of APELLES or RAPHAEL to
paint a God bounding across the Ægean sea,
in any manner, that he shall not appear as
like a man skipping over a kennel; as one
egg is like another. An image altogether
mean and ungodlike.

Wherein then consists the sublimity of
this passage? Probably in words only; and
that any effort of the mind, to turn those
words into imagery, would give it, instead of
pleasure, that uneasiness, which it suffers
during the restless slumbers of a fever. The
human mind cannot create any thing; it can
only reflect, like a looking-glass, but a looking-glass where the images remain after the
objects are removed: and the pleasure we
receive from the works of art, either in po-

poetry that did honour to her author. LONGINUS,
however, seems rather to side with her, as in his com-
mendation of HOMER's Neptune, he has quoted some
lines that precede, and some that follow this passage,
without taking notice of it. So great a contrariety of
sentiment amongst celebrated judges, ought to convince
us of the insufficiency of meer TASTE; and the necessity of looking for some rule, by which it may be
directed.

etry or painting, is greater or less, according as the images produced by the artist do
more or less resemble those contained in
this repository † : Or, as POPE says,

> *True wit is nature to advantage drest,*
> *Which oft was thought, but ne'er so well*
> *exprest.*
> *Something whose truth, convinc'd, at sight*
> *we find,*
> *That gives us back the image of our mind.*

And the greatest poet, whenever he mistakes
the bounds of his art so much, as to endea-

---

† Mr. ADDISON, whose papers upon *The Pleasures of
the Imagination* deserve great encomiums, has, nevertheless, lost much of the consistency which might have
appeared on that subject, by not establishing a constant
attachment to TRUTH, as the leading and inseparable
principle in all the works of art. For instance, he
says, N°. 421. *Those different allusions are but so many
different manners of similitude; and, that they may please
the imagination, the likeness ought to be very exact,* or
*very agreeable; as we love to see a picture where the re-
semblance is just, or the posture and air graceful.*

He is here as unfortunate in his illustration, as in his
principle; for the *agreeable*, in those cases, cannot be
separated from the *exact*: and a posture, in painting,
must be a *just resemblance* of what is graceful in nature, before it can hope to be esteem'd *graceful*.

Part vour to reprefent to others, what the eye
I. hath not feen, nor the ear heard; altho'
he may flatter himfelf, like BAYES, that his
attempt is *great*, yet the application of
the rule, fuggefted in this Section *, will
never

* I fufpect that HORACE had an eye to this method
of criticifm in the commencement of his art of poetry.

Humano capiti cervicem pictor equinam
Jungere fi velit, et varias inducere plumas,
Undique collatis membris, ut turpiter atrum
Definat in pifcem muiier formofa fuperne;
Spectatum admiffi rifum teneatis amici?
Credite, Pifones, ifti tabulæ fore librum
Perfimilem, cujus, velut ægri fomnia, vanæ
Fingentur fpecies; ut nec pes, nec caput uni
Reddatur formæ. Pictoribus atque poetis
Quidlibet audendi femper fuit æqua poteftas.
Scimus; et hanc veniam petimufque damufque viciffim.
Sed non ut placidis coeant immitia; non ut
Serpentes avibus geminentur, tigribus agni.

Here, as in many other places, that excellent critic
illuftrates the beauties and defects of poetry, by allufions made to painting; which he is generally thought
to do, only becaufe poetry happen'd to be his theme
at that time; and that, had he been to treat of painting, he would have *vice verfa* illuftrated painting, by
allufions made to the operations of the fifter art.
There may be perhaps, another reafon affigned that
may make the allufions in the cafe actually before us
more

never fail to convince the judicious of its being monstrous and ridiculous.

more proper and conducive than if the case were re-vers'd. The use of allusions, as has been already hint-ed in this Essay, is to establish obscure or dubious truths, by the aid of similar truths that are more obvious. Lines and colours are of a more determined nature, and strike the mind more immediately than words ; which, before they can produce any effect, must be form'd by the mind itself, into pictures ; and conse-quently require a more tedious, and more difficult pro-cess. This HORACE himself expresses, in another part of the same work, where speaking of theatrical repre-sentations, which are a mixture of poetry and painting, he says,

Segnius irritant animos demissa per aurem,
Quam quæ sunt oculis subjecta fidelibus, et quæ
Ipse sibi tradit spectator.

Upon this consideration it is, that he makes use of a similitude borrowed from the art of painting, which condemns the extravagancies and incongruities of cer-tain poets, by shewing that the like would be in a painter unpardonable and ridiculous.

The hopes of finding something to confirm my con-jecture concerning the meaning of this passage of HO-RACE, induced me to look into many of his commen-tators, particularly DACIER and SANADON, but I found nothing there that pointed towards it. I observed how-ever at the same time, that those learned Frenchmen, in their translations, had entirely passed over the word

F

æqua,

PART *æqua*, which is join'd to *poteſtas* in the 10th line; and
II. that the former underſtood *petimuſque damuſque viciſſim,*
to relate to poets and critics. In this he appears to have
very much miſtaken his author's meaning; as there had
been no mention at all of critics, and that it would have
been very abſurd in HORACE to have ſaid, that critics
claim'd a right to boldneſs and invention, that put them
upon a level with poets. I will therefore endeavour
to give a general ſenſe of thoſe 13 lines, in a manner that will make them conſiſtent with the truth of
things, with one another, and probably with the inten
tion of the author.

" If to a human face a painter ſhould join the neck
" of a horſe, with wings of various colours; collecting
" in like manner, the other members from different
" animals, ſo that the breaſt of a fair woman ſhould
" terminate in a fiſh's tail: would not you, who are
" connoiſſeurs, think the ſpectacle extremely ridicu-
" lous? And yet, believe me, nothing can be more
" akin to this picture, than a poem, whoſe unaccount-
" able images, like a ſick man's dreams, are ſuch,
" that no one part has any manner of relation to
" another. Painters and poets have always had an
" equal right to be bold in their compoſitions.
" This we know, and it is by this equal right, that we
" poets muſt not dare to write, what a painter would
" not dare to paint; nor does the painter, on the other
" hand, expect any indulgence, but what he is willing
" to grant to his brother poet. But this indulgence
" never extends itſelf to thoſe, who loſe ſight of na-
" ture; nor allows either of the artiſts to introduce
" the dove ſporting with the ſerpent, nor the lamb
" with the tiger."

AN

AN
ESSAY
ON
RIDICULE.

PART. II.

LAUGHTER, as I have before observed, *is the consequence of Ridicule*,
from whence it receives its name;
but it is proper to take notice, that it is
only a symptom, and not its distinguishing character. For laughter is produced upon many occasions, where nothing like Ridicule is applied. A slap on the face may
raise a laugh in the by-standers; but if they
were to burst their sides, it has no more
pretension to Ridicule, than it has to *pa-*

thetic

PART *thetic eloquence* *. It is reported of a man
II. once eminent for his love of the public, that
he was never known to laugh in the courſe of
his life, but once ; and that was, upon ſeeing his brother fall and break his arm. And
there is nothing more common, than to obſerve people in health and affluence, laugh
and ſneer at the bodily infirmities, weakneſs
of intellects, thread-bare cloaths, and other
marks of the diſtreſs or poverty of thoſe,
who accidentally come in their way. Is this
Ridicule ? Thoſe refin'd philoſophers, who
have diſcover'd in Man *moral feelings* and
inſtincts, which are to ſerve him as a *criterion* of right and wrong, and are ſatisfied to
receive this into the number; much good may
it do them. There is great reaſon to believe,
that JUVENAL would join with me in ſay-
ing, *Hæc noſtri pars* PESSIMA *ſenſus* ; and that
there are few greater ſymptoms of moral
turpitude in human nature. And yet my
Lord SHAFTSBURY's antagoniſt, by making
Contempt and *Ridicule* ſynonomous terms,
has employed ſome pages of his book in
proving, that this inhuman folly can never

* See the laſt Note of Sect. II.

be

be the teſt of truth †. Men of the beſt PART
ſenſe will never fail to confound themſelves II.
and others, when they are not at pains, by
definitions and examples, to aſcertain the
meaning of their terms. When we ſee Ridicule underſtood to be *pathetic eloquence* in
one page, in another *contempt* ; why not perjury, a gooſe, a gridiron, or a cheſt of
drawers ? By ſuch ſkilful management any
one thing may be proved to have none of
its own properties, but all the properties of
any thing elſe, to the great advancement of
knowledge.

A man who even laughs at folly or vice,
which are certainly the objects of pity or de-
teſtation, to ſound and liberal minds, gives
us as bad a ſample of his morals as of his
underſtanding. How comes it then, that a
Ridicule of thoſe very follies and vices is followed by a laugh or ſmile from the moſt
humane ? To me it appears very plain, that
the laugh, in this caſe, is not a laugh ariſing
from the contempt of the perſon or thing
ridiculed ; but a laugh of pleaſure, from the

† *Eſſays on the Characteriſticks*, Sect. V. at the beginning.

art itſelf, and of applauſe to the artiſt. There are ſome philoſophers, who have derived laughter from pride, and from the pleaſure which we receive in comparing our own ſtrength with the infirmities of others. I know not upon what they ground this opinion, and it is foreign to my preſent ſubject to enter deep into the enquiry. But I am throughly convinced, from many obſervations, external and internal, that the motives I have here aſſign'd are true in the caſe of Ridicule, and perhaps it may ſerve as a hint for further diſcoveries. Why ſhould we indulge ourſelves in meer conjectures, to the diſadvantage of the human heart? Perhaps the ſneer and laugh of contempt which we ſo often with abhorrence obſerve, is not natural; but only affected, and put on to ſhew ſuperior parts and diſcernment. It is moſt commonly to be ſeen, not ſo much among the proud and ill-natured, as among the empty, the half-bred, and the half-witted; who I fancy are often led into this mean and monkey-like practice, by hearing men of acknowledg'd wit celebrated for *laughing at perſons and things*; which they take literally, not knowing that by theſe words is meant,

expoſing

exposing those persons and things in a new
and artful manner, and thereby exciting laughter in all those whom they thus entertain,
while they themselves preserve the greatest
seriousness and modesty of countenance.

Thus much was necessary to premise, before we enter upon the second kind of Ridicule, which consists in the bare *represen-*
tation of what is improper in manners or ac-
tions. It may be stiled, SIMPLE, DIRECT, or
UNREFLECTED RIDICULE; and if it comes
under the description of the *art, which shews*
that to be ridiculous which is imagined to be so,
it is only by bringing the ridiculous out of ob-
scurity, and placing it in open day-light.
And, indeed, as POPE says,

Vice is a creature of so vile a mien,
That, to-be hated, needs but to be seen.

For this sort of Ridicule is one of those
which ARISTOTLE, in his *Poetics*, calls *mi-*
mic arts; and deriving all its merit from its
obvious likeness, to what it proposes to represent, has not the least pretence to be re-

F 4

ceived

PART II. ceived as a teſt of truth; with whatſoever uſefulneſs it may be otherwiſe attended. It may be divided into ſeveral branches; but chiefly into the NARRATIVE, GRAPHIC, and DRAMATIC. I ſhall exemplify all theſe ſeparately; beginning with the GRAPHIC, or what is produced by the painter.

And of all thoſe artiſts, who have employed their pencils in repreſenting what they thought ridiculous in the manners of men, I know of none, who deſerves to be mentioned upon this occaſion, but the incomparable HOGARTH. Others there are, Dutch, Flemiſh, French, and Italians, who have painted life in all its calamitous circumſtances, of poverty, oppreſſion, bodily ſickneſs, and deformity. But ARISTOTLE *, and common ſenſe have long ago told us, that theſe things are not ridiculous; and to all, but the unfeeling, are the objects of com-

* Η ΔΕ ΚΩΜΩΔΙΑ ΕΣΤΙΝ, ΩΣΠΕΡ ΕΙΠΟΜΕΝ, ΜΙΜΗΣΙΣ ΦΑΥΛΟΤΕΡΩΝ ΜΕΝ, ΟΥ ΜΕΝΤΟΙ ΚΑΤΑ ΠΑΣΑΝ ΚΑΚΙΑΝ, ΑΛΛΑ ΤΟΥ ΑΙΣΧΡΟΥ ΕΣΤΙ ΤΟ ΓΕΛΟΙΟΝ ΜΟΡΙΟΝ. ΤΟ ΓΑΡ ΓΕΛΟΙΟΝ ΕΣΤΙΝ ΑΜΑΡΤΗΜΑ ΤΙ, ΚΑΙ ΑΙΣΧΟΣ ΑΝΩΔΥΝΟΝ, ΚΑΙ ΟΥ ΦΘΑΡΤΙΚΟΝ. *Ariſt. Poetic.* cap. 5.

paſſion,

paſſion, and not of laughter. It was re-
ſerved for our ingenious countryman, to expoſe upon immortal canvaſs the faſhionable
follies, vices and affectations of his cotem-
poraries. He has gone ſtill farther, and by
producing his repreſentations in serieſes, and
ſhewing the frightful, tho natural tendency
of thoſe follies, has adminiſter'd one of the
moſt practical incitements to virtue, and ful-
filled the moſt material duty of a moral
philoſopher; and that by a language, which
all men underſtand, and which makes the
quickeſt and ſtrongeſt impreſſion upon their
minds *.

This is employing a very extraordinary
talent in a way, which greatly deſerves the
thanks of the public. Let us ſee next,
whether this talent, like many other good
things, may not be abuſed in its turn; and
render'd hurtful to ſociety, by ridiculing
thoſe actions which are innocent or praiſe-
worthy.

* See the laſt Section of Part I. with the notes upon
it.

But

But when we confider the nature of this fort of Ridicule, ever fo flightly, it will appear, that whenever it takes effect at all, it is always from its being *true Ridicule*; that is, *giving a reprefentation of what is truly ridiculous*. And fuch is its fimplicity, that there never can be any fallacy attending it, except by the means of a downright lie, in attributing an action or circumftance, in itfelf ridiculous, to a perfon, to whom it does not belong.

For inftance, fuppofe Mr. HOGARTH, to expofe the odioufnefs of drunkennefs and quarrelling in men of important ftations, fhould paint two magiftrates in their fur-gowns fprawling on the floor, and batter-ing one another, with countenances that breathed *fcoundrel* and *rafcal* as emphatically as if the words flowed in labels out of their mouths; fhould HOGARTH, I fay, deline-ate fuch a midnight converfation, with all the natural circumftances of torn cravats, fpilt claret, and broken tobacco-pipes, which his lively fancy would prefently fuggeft to him, the piece could not fail of being ufeful as well as comical. But fhould he, to ferve

the

the vile purpoſes of a party, or to gratify a PAR.
private grudge, (I beg his pardon for the ſup- II.
poſition,) ſhould he write under theſe figures,
*This is Mr.------ and this is Mr.------*uſing
the names of two men moſt eminent for
their ſobriety and diſcretion ; or, if inſtead
of writing, he ſhould inſert the features of
thoſe worthy magiſtrates, the general Ridicule would be ſtill as juſt as it was before;
and the artiſt would receive, at York or
Carliſle, his uſual tribute of praiſe: but
they, who were better inſtructed in the affairs
of London, would be ſhocked at the performance, and would withdraw from the
author that eſteem, which the reſt of his conduct had ſo juſtly acquired.

This, I will venture to ſay, is the plain
ſtate of the caſe, with regard to the abuſes,
that may happen in all the different ſpecies
of REPRESENTATIVE Ridicule. And it is particularly the caſe of SOCRATES, which has
been ſo often quoted to the diſadvantage of
Ridicule in general, altho moſt unjuſtly;
as it will eaſily appear, that SOCRA-
TES fell not a ſacrifice, as is pretended, to
wit

wit and Ridicule, but to falſhood and miſ-
representation.

Thoſe who are acquainted with the character of that great man ; his moderation
and univerſal benevolence; his juſtneſs and
elegance of thought; his courage and un-
ſhaken fidelity in the defence of his country;
and his conſtant endeavour to render all men
as moderate, as virtuous, and as uſeful members of ſociety as himſelf : muſt be ſatisfied
that ſuch a character had nothing in it, that
was ridiculous, and that it was entirely out
of the reach of Ridicule. Of this the conduct
of ARISTOPHANES was likewiſe a proof. He
was very ſenſible of the difficulties, he had
to encounter ; he knew, that his talents could
not be employed with ſucceſs againſt any
thing, that was not ridiculous in itſelf; and
therefore took advantage of the ignorance of
the multitude, already prejudiced by the
heathen prieſts, and the leaders of a faction ;
and exhibited to them a SOCRATES of his
own creation, ridiculous to an extreme degree ; and in every reſpect the oppoſite of
him, whom it was ſaid to repreſent. If the
event of this repreſentation proved fatal to
that

that excellent philofopher, we muſt blame PART the villany, not the wit of the poet ; and we **II.** muſt not lay to the charge of Ridicule a mis- fortune, which will equally attend the moſt ſerious indictment, when it happens to be founded upon facts, that are either feigned or unfairly ſtated.

So much for the GRAPHIC and DRAMA- TIC *.

Of the NARRATIVE Ridicule there are in- ſtances in the *Characters of* THEOPHRASTUS, LA BRUYERE, PETRONIUS, *Memoirs of the houſe of* Brandenburgh, *&c.*

* Under the article of *dramatic Ridicule*, may be properly put thoſe philological pieces of Ridicule, which are meant to expoſe affectation, awkwardneſs, and bad taſte in writing and diſcourſe, and which have been often, and ſucefsfully employed by the beſt critics. Of this ſort are the *Lexiphanes* and other pieces of LUCIAN ; the *Limoſin* and other chapters of RABELAIS ; SWIFT's *Memoirs of P. P.* His *Tritical eſſay on the faculties of the mind* ; *Polite converſation* ; *Meditations on a broom-ſtick*, &c. and, like all the different ſpecies of this kind of Ri- dicule, are capable of being miſapplied, by having the names of perſons affixed to them, whom perhaps they reſemble not at all, or only in part.

Theſe

PART
II.

These species of mimic Ridicule are sometimes to be found single, sometimes compounded; and often acquire a new name by the composition. As,

The THEATRICAL Ridicule, which is a compound of the *graphic* and *dramatic*; the actor performing the function both of the painter and poet. This sometimes likewise receives the narrative Ridicule; as, when an actor, in the character of Sir *John Falstaff*, gives a description of his recruits in his march to Coventry.

Sometimes the NARRATIVE Ridicule, is interspersed with the DRAMATIC, as in the *Trimalchio* of PETRONIUS, *Payfan parvenu* of Marivaux, *Joseph Andrews*, *Pompey the little*, &c. †

It

† *Don Quixote*, for some things, may be ranked amongst those *representations of real life*, as in the character of *Sancho*, and others. There are likewise strokes of the *argumentative Ridicule* in the character of *Parson Adams*, and other characters in those instructing novels written by Mr. FIELDING. The intention of the present *Essay*, is not to enumerate all the different ways

It would be endleſs to relate the various Part ſhapes in which this representative Ridi- II. cule has appeared; but they all agree ſo much in the general character of being *pictures of life and manners*, and are ſo much the ſame in their nature and properties, that there does not appear occaſion for more than one ſhort ſection to explain the whole theory of them. It is a ſort of Ridicule, that may be of uſe in giving lively impreſſions of known truths; but whoever is at the pains to prove, that it can never be a teſt of truth, will have the pleaſure of arguing without the trouble of an opponent; ſince it never was applied in ſubjects of ſpeculation, and, even in its own province of repreſenting the de- formities of life and manners, cannot prove its own juſtneſs, with regard to the ap- plication, but by extraneous evidence and aſſiſtance.

There is reaſon however to ſuſpect, from ſeveral paſſages in the *Eſſays upon the charac-*

ways, in which the different kinds and ſpecies of Ridi- cule may be mixed, but only to give ſome general hints of thoſe principles, by which a more exact diſcuſſion may be made.

teriſticks,

teriſticks, that, while the author ſpeaks of Ridicule in general, he only means this MIMIC ſort, as in page 46. *Again, it may be obſerved, that the conſequences of Ridicule, with regard to ſpeculative inſtruction and enquiry, are of a very different nature from thoſe which relate to morals and action: to the firſt it muſt ever be an enemy; but to the latter it may be an enemy or a friend, according as it is fairly or diſhoneſtly applied.* If he means, I ſay, only the MIMIC Ridicule, his aſſertion has been ſufficiently confirmed and exemplified in this ſection. The ſubject is too ſimple to admit of any difference of opinion concerning it; and cannot, in itſelf, incur either praiſe or blame. The only Ridicule, whoſe legality is worth the diſputing, is that which has been treated of in the firſt part of this *Eſſay*. It was that alone, which could give give riſe to this controverſy; being a weapon often uſed by the learned and ingenious, who never ſeem in fact, as has been obſerved by Lord SHAFTSBURY, to have queſtioned its lawfulneſs, unleſs when it happened to be in the enemy's hands.

To

To conclude. It has been often recom-
mended to thofe, who take upon them the
inftruction of mankind, that they fhould
convey their leffons in fuch a way, as might
render them *agreeable* as well as *ufeful:* tho'
this was meant, like putting fugar into a
bitter potion, only to render it more palatable, and to be more willingly fwallowed by
the patient; without its being looked upon
as any part of the medicine itfelf. But, if
what has been fet forth in the firft part of
this *Effay,* with regard to the ingredients
which compofe Ridicule and pleafantry in
writing, is found to be true; if *appeals to
experience* are the beft teft of truth; if thofe
appeals are *leaft fubject to fallacy,* when
made to *facts the moft vulgar* and *familiar;*
if in the moft *ferious* queftions, fuch wherein
the welfare of mankind is chiefly interefted,
*the entertainment rifes in proportion to the
familiarity of the known truths,* by the application of which any falfhood in thofe
important points is detected: if, I fay, thefe
things are fo, then it will be eafy to perceive
a more then accidental connection betwixt

Part the *utile* and the *dulce*; it will be eaſy to
II. perceive, that in ſpeculative, as well as in
active life, *the ways of Wiſdom are* really
ways of pleaſantneſs; and that a true philoſopher, that is, a man of candour, ſenſe
and knowledge, has a better chance than
ordinary of improving the underſtandings
of thoſe with whom he converſes, at the very
inſtant that he makes them laugh.

FINIS.

A

LETTER

TO THE

RIGHT HONOURABLE

THE

EARL of ———

Concerning the AFFAIR of

Elizabeth Canning.

By a CLERGYMAN.

LONDON,

Printed for T. SEDDON at *Homer*'s Head in the
Poultry. MDCCLIII.

[Price one Shilling.]

THE

EDITOR's *Advertisement.*

THE Nobleman to whom this
Letter was addreſs'd, thinking
it of general Utility, has permitted it
to be printed. And, as he is ſenſible
of the Regard which the Gentleman
who wrote it pays to the Publick
Good, he is under no Apprehenſion
of his diſapproving of the Publication,
tho done without his Conſent.

For the Eaſe and Satisfaction of
the Reader, the Editor has put Re-
ferences, at the bottom of the Pages,
to the ſeveral Paſſages in the Pamphlets alluded to in this Letter, and
has likewiſe inſerted ſome whole Pa-
ragraphs from the News-Papers, &c.
that are now difficult to be met with.

A
LETTER

TO THE

RIGHT HONOURABLE

THE

EARL of ———

My LORD,

I Hope your Lordſhip received the letter I ſent laſt Friday, by *Richard* along with Lady ———'s tea and dimmity. I ſhould have given you then, as you probably expected, my opinion concerning the affair of *Elizabeth Canning*; but I fancy the firſt ſight of this, which, if I may believe the heap of memorandums that lye upon the table before me, will have more the ſize of a book than a letter, will make a very plauſible excuſe for my delay. Indeed, my dear Lord, there is nothing I undertake with more alacrity and chearfulneſs

B   than

than whatever tends to your amuſement, eſpecially when I perceive it to be connected with your inſtruction, which was many years my ſole employment, and is ſtill part of the duty of my peculiar function: but my eyes are now ſo weak, that I can neither read or write any thing without frequent intermiſſions.

The ſtory, as your Lordſhip obſerves, is very puzzling, and ſo it appears to the inhabitants of this great city, where it has been the univerſal ſubject of controverſy for many weeks, and the majority ſeem ſtill to be of opinion that the firſt account was the truth, if we may judge by the late proceedings of the grand jury, of which your news papers I ſuppoſe have given you the particulars.

It is but lately, that I myſelf have had any knowledge of this affair. The melancholy event which brought me to town, hindered me from attending to what was doing in it, and perhaps I ſhould to this hour have remained in ignorance, had not my attention been awakened by ſeeing a

pam-

pamphlet advertifed on the fubject by Mr. *Fielding*.

Your Lordfhip knows the value I fet upon every thing that is written by that author, who has fucceeded fo well in every fubject he has undertaken, either of bufinefs or pleafantry; and I with great reafon expected one or other of thefe from the twelvepenny worth I faw advertifed. And, perhaps there are none of his performances that more difcover the ingenuity of the man of wit, the diftinctnefs of the lawyer, or the politenefs and candour of the gentleman.

But while I admired the ftile and compofition of this pamphlet, and the ingenious, and at the fame time unadorned method, in which Mr. *Fielding* defended the caufe of *Canning*, I could not help being furprized to find upon what flight grounds he and many other fenfible men, had founded their belief of her veracity; and that they fhould be fatisfied with evidence that feems to be in no manner adequate to the nature of the facts meant to

be

be proved by it: especially when a life is concerned, of which our laws and customs are in most cases extremely tender.

It is reported about town, as you may see by the news papers, that there are several evidences to the *alibi* of the gypsy *Squires*, and other counter evidences: but as I know nothing certain concerning them, I shall confine myself, in the opinion you do me the honour to ask, to the proofs that were produced before and at the trial of *Squires*, as they appear in the *Sessions paper*, Mr. Fielding's *state of the case*, and other *papers* published by the friends of *Canning*, not thinking any other proof necessary to convince those who are unprejudiced that her relation is false. Yet in doing this I should be sorry to be suspected of meaning any reflection upon the Justices, Judges, or Jury who concurred in the condemnation of *Squires*; since if I should prove beyond doubt my whole assertion, it will amount to no more than to shew the power of prepossession upon honest, disinterested and compassionate

fionate minds, and how cautious we ought
to be in allowing any degree of weight to
perfonal credit, and character, in oppofition to the general evidence of things.

Mr. *Fielding* very candidly owns, that
there is the *higheft degree of improbability*
attending the circumftances related by *Elizabeth Canning*, and only infifts upon their
not amounting to an impoffibility. He is too
much a philofopher, and too much a mafter of language to mean any more by a
fact's being *poffible*, than that it implies
no contradiction in itfelf, and in that fenfe
no doubt the ftory of *Canning* is *poffible*;
and fo it would have been if fhe had gone
a little farther, and faid fhe had been dead
and buried during the time fhe was miffing.
For this is *poffible*, and all that we could
object to the relation of it is, that it is
extremely *unufual* for dead people to return
to life, and therefore we are not warranted
to believe it without fome proof *unufually*
ftrong.

Thus to bring a fact within the compafs
of poffibility, there is nothing required but

that

that it ſhould not contradict itſelf; but
to make it probable, it is likewiſe required
that it ſhould not be contradictory to
ordinary experience: for in proportion to
the ſeveral degrees in which it is removed from common experience, it acquires
an appearance of falſhood, and to entitle
it to belief, muſt be ſupported by evidence
apparently true, to as great or greater degree
than the fact which it means to prove, is
apparently falſe.

This, your Lordſhip knows, is the general
and leading principle in all enquiries concerning probable evidence; and upon this
principle therefore give me leave to examine, firſt the ſtory of *Canning*, and then
the proof of it, weighing one againſt the
other.

Firſt, as to the ſtory itſelf, it is ſo far
from being like any thing that was ever
heard or ſeen before, that to relate it as
a truth, looks like an inſult upon the
common ſenſe of mankind, as will appear
to any one, who will try to anſwer the
following queries.

Was

Was it ever known that any plurality of human creatures were actuated by the same kind of delirium, or ever concurred unanimously for any time in the same passion, caprice, or unaccountable whim? or was it ever known that any plurality of human creatures ever acted conjunctly but from vulgar and obvious motives of interest, safety, or pleasure?

To be more particular, was it ever known that two footpads, after having committed a robbery for which they were both liable to be hanged, instead of flying from the watch, or *battering the skull of the robbed person with their clubs*, to prevent the appearance in judgment against them, ever made the robbed person a partner in their flight?

Was it ever known that two ruffians after having committed a robbery, and as they had great reason to believe a murder*, did ever persist in carrying

---

* We apprehend the author alludes to her being knocked down and continuing some hours in a fainting fit; which, to ignorant men, and in the dark, must bear a very great resemblance to death.

or

or dragging the carcafe of the murdered perfon ten miles, with much fatigue and hazard of being met; without its being poffible for imagination to fuggeft any benefit, they could propofe to themfelves by this enterprize?

Was it ever read in any of the records of iniquity, that an old bawd and her affociates were fo ignorant of their own trade, as to think of winning a young girl to the ways of lewdnefs by hunger and cold; or to raife the price of her beauty by ftarving her black in the face?

Was it ever known that a number of people, no lefs than nine*, of bad characters, and equally involved in guilt which already amounted to felony, and was verging every hour towards murder, were fo quiet and unanimous in their cruel proceedings for the fpace of 28 days?

Was it ever known that fuch a number of wretches ever chofe, for the fcene of fuch a tragedy, a room opening into the kitchen of a public bawdy houfe, upon a moft

* See Mr. *Fielding*'s pamphlet, p. 45.

pub-

public highway, with a horſepond under its window, without any guard, or the ſmalleſt attention to the priſoner, whoſe dying groan might have brought them all to the gallows?

Was it ever known that a whole ſet of people guilty of ſuch crimes, remained quietly to be ſeized by the officers of juſtice, two days after they knew their guilt was diſcovered; and knew at the ſame time that the badneſs of their characters would make the ſlighteſt evidence be ſufficient for their conviction?

Any one of the circumſtances, alluded to in the foregoing queries, would be ſufficient to throw an air of falſhood upon a ſtory, altho' likely in every other particular. What ſhall we ſay, then, of a ſtory which is compoſed altogether of ſuch circumſtances? Nothing, but that either the circumſtances are falſe, or that God Almighty has created a ſet of people at *Enfield Waſh*, totally different in all their deſires, fears, paſſions, and apprehenſions, from the reſt of mankind.

I ſay

I fay nothing of the improbability of the girl's returning ten miles, through a train of open inns, and gentlemens houfes, without feeking relief from her hunger, reft for her weaknefs, or protection from her murderers, who fhe had the ftrongeft reafon to believe were hard in pur- fuit of her; becaufe, there are found fuch particularities of temper, and underftand- ing in particular perfons, as to account for almoft any deviation in them from thofe general laws of human nature, by which large focieties are influenced with much certainty and uniformity.

For a like reafon I will omit troubling your Lordfhip, with a repetition of the various phyfical improbabilities, which you have already been informed of by feveral of the pamphlets I have fent you, particularly by Mr. *Dodd*'s; that I may come to a new fet of improbabilities, that have been hitherto overlooked. Thefe are not, like the reft, improbabilities, arifing from what *Canning* told of her ftory, but from what fhe did not tell.

To

To explain what I mean by this, it is neceſſary, that I ſhould give you a few lines upon the theory of lying; an art, of which, in your moſt infant years, you never knew the practice. And ſurely, if a man were to thank the Giver of all good, for any one bleſſing more than another, it ought to be for having beſtowed upon him a heart utterly un-inclined to deceit, with an underſtanding to conceive the miſerable conſequences of it. For of all the trades under the ſun, that of a liar, who expects to be believed, is the moſt difficult. This ariſes from many cauſes, but I ſhall only mention one, as it is neceſſary for my preſent purpoſe: and that is the difficulty of managing with regard to circumſtances in general; which it is equally dangerous to inſert, or to let alone. If a lie is made circumſtantial, with the names and deſcriptions of perſons, places, dates, and other furniture, it will be plauſible and gain immediate credit; but then every one of thoſe circumſtances, which at firſt gave it

ⁿthority,

authority, may administer means of trace-
ing, and discovering its falshood.

If to avoid this, the relater gives no
names of persons, places, or particularities, the story will justly be look'd upon
as a lie from the beginning.

Upon this principle arises those queries
concerning the story of *Canning*, which I
hinted above, such as,

How came she to be so bare in her relation of the various incidents, that must
have happen'd between *Moorfields* and *Enfield*; during which journey, there must
have been many things both said and done
by the two ruffians she described? To answer this, she has told us, she was in a fit;
and perhaps it had been prudent in her
to have said, her fit continued all the
time she remained in *Wells*'s house. If
she had, it would have only made a new
physical oddity, to be accounted for by
Mr. *Dodd*, and I should have had no
more questions of this sort to ask. But
unhappily she has not left herself that
means of evasion.

How

How came it then, that fhe liv'd 28 days in *Wells*'s houfe, without being able to give the leaft account of what paffed in it: altho' fhe had an opportunity, through a large hole, to fee and hear every thing that was done in the kitchen; a place which, at that time of the year, muft have been the moft frequented in the houfe, and where there muft have always been light to difcover to her their motions, while the darknefs of the hay-loft would always take away all fear of her curiofity being obferv'd ?

How comes it, that fhe gave no account of *Fortune Natus* and his wife *Sarah*, who, by the evidence of *V. Hall*, ftill urged to be true by her and her friends, lay every night in that kitchen ?

To abridge the enquiry, and reduce it to a fhorter catechifm. What happend to *Elizabeth Canning*, during the fix hours and a half that fhe was upon the road betwixt *Moorfields* and *Enfield* ? Her own account will inform your Lordfhip: NOTHING.

What

What happen'd in the whole hour she remain'd in mother *Wells's* kitchen ? Next to Nothing.

What happen'd to her during the 28 days that she was confined in mother *Wells's* house ? Nothing.

What happen'd to her during the six hours that she was upon the road from *Enfield* to her mother's house ? Nothing.

Never sure was there a history that stood less in need of abridgment. But altho' we should muster out a catalogue of improbabilities attending this affair, more numerous than that of the stars, still, as Mr. *Fielding* very justly observes, there is no impossibility in it; and altho' utterly incredible in itself, may become the object of belief, by proper evidence, that may make the belief of its being true, more easy than the belief of its being false.

Accordingly we find, that some of *Canning's* advocates have endeavoured to oppose improbability against improbability; and have urged, that supposing her story

to

to be falfe, we are put to as great a difficulty to account for her motives, as we
are to account for thofe of *Squires*, and
her affociates, when we fuppofe it to be
true.

This proceeds, in great meafure, from
the fuperficial, and hear-fay manner, in
which they receive the ftory from one
another, without looking narrowly into
the original and authentick accounts
of it.

It would be extremely diverting to your
Lordfhip, to hear fome of thofe good
people, puzzling themfelves with difficulties of their own raifing; and afking
queftions, which can admit of no anfwers,
but what have much the air of crofs purpofes. For inftance,

How could Canning *be at mother* Wells's
houfe upon any other occafion, without
Wells, *and the reft, being able to give an*
account of her, when it was their intereft
fo to do?

Anfwer. She never had been in *Wells's*
houfe.

If

If she never had been in Wells's *house, how came she so exactly to describe it?*

Answer. She did not describe it at all.

How could she fix upon a place so far from home, and where it appears she never had been before?

Answer. She did not fix upon it at all.

How could a young girl of a good character, be so wantonly cruel, as to form a design, of taking away the lives of so many people, who had never injured her?

Answer. She never had any design against them, or their lives.

How could so young, and simple a girl contrive so artful a story?

Answer. It is not an artful, but on the contrary, an exceeding stupid story. An artful story, is such a story as *Tom Jones*, where the incidents are so various, and yet so consistent with themselves, and with nature, that the more the reader is acquainted with nature, the more he is deceived into a belief of its being true; and is with difficulty recall'd from that belief

by

by the author's confeſſion from time to time of its being all a fiction. But what is there plauſible in the adventures of *Enfield Waſh?* What is there ſtrange or poetically fancied in the incidents of *robbing, knocking down — cry'd out murder — ſtopt my mouth with a handkerchief — you bitch, why don't you go faſter? — carrying to a bawdy houſe — offer of fine cloaths —— cut your throat if you ſtir?* Such is the *variety* of theſe incidents, which owe all their *ſtrangeneſs* to the ſenſeleſs manner in which they have been, with reſpect to time and place, jumbled together.

There is nothing *ſurpriſing* in ſuch ſtories, except their meeting with any degree of belief; and that ſurpriſe commonly ceaſes, whenever we ſet ourſelves coolly to examine into their origin, and trace them to their fountain head.

A wild *Indian,* ſuddenly landed in *England,* would think the firſt houſe he ſaw of four ſtories high, a work more than human. But after ſtanding by a bricklayer for half an hour, and ſeeing

C   that

that this ſtupendous fabric was mounted up only by laying one brick quietly by the ſide of another, his wonder ceaſes, and, inſtead of four ſtories, he would not be ſurpriſed at a houſe of four and twenty.

Let us therefore, my Lord, endeavour to follow the affair of *Canning*, brick by brick, and ſee whether we cannot, if not truly, at leaſt probably and eaſily, account for every ſtep of her conduct, and like-wiſe for all the belief that attended her relation, without being obliged to give the leaſt credit to any one circumſtance contain'd in it; each of which, as I have already ſhewn, carries the word L I E, in great letters upon its forehead.

In doing this I ſhall diſtinguiſh, by a different character, what I relate as cer-tain facts, from thoſe conjectures of my own that are neceſſary for their con-nection; that you may yourſelf judge how ſimple and few thoſe conjectures are, and that I may not ſeem to impoſe my own perſonal credit and opinion upon

I   your

your Lordſhip, while I am endeavouring to inſpire you with a diffidence for perſonal credit and opinion in general.

First, then, it is certain that *E. Canning was miſſing from the 1st of January at nine 'till the 29th at ten o'clock at night, when ſhe came to her mother's houſe.* Where ſhe was during this interval of time, or in what manner employed, we do not pretend to have diſcover'd, for if that could be done our conjectures would be loſt in certainty, and there would be an end of all reaſoning upon the ſubject. But hitherto no intelligence of that ſort has been receiv'd. In the mean time it is ſufficient, that there are various ways of employing a month, beſides walking up and down in mother *Wells's* hay-loft. And if my good friend Sir ———, and the Doctor, ſhould inſiſt upon its being as difficult to conceive her being any where elſe, as to believe the truth of what ſhe relates; and that no conjecture can account for the miſerable ſtate in which, it is ſaid, ſhe return'd; it may

C 2   not

not be amiſs to hint to them that there
are ſuch diſtempers as lyings-in and miſ-
carriages, to which young ſervant-maids
of eighteen are very much ſubject; diſtempers that will hold them as long, and
reduce them as low as has been related of
E. Canning, eſpecially if attended and
nurſed in the manner we may eaſily ſuppoſe her to have been. It may not be
amiſs to hint, that thirteen ſhillings and
ſix-pence, with the ſale of a gown and pair
of ſtays, is hardly more than ſufficient to
defray the expences of ſuch an operation;
even altho' no part of it was expended in
a chriſtening, a wet nurſe, or a coffin,
which, not to continue any idea of horror
in your Lordſhip's imagination, might
have been all provided by that moſt humane inſtitution, the Foundling-Hoſpital.
Our friends may perhaps aſk: How comes
it that the people with whom ſhe paſſed
this month do not make the diſcovery,
when by letting it alone they ſacrificed the
life of an innocent perſon? But this is
eaſily accounted for, by ſuppoſing them
involved

involved with *Canning* in some guilt,
which makes their own preservation de-
pend upon their secrecy, or that their
friendship for her makes them prefer her
safety and character to the life of an old
gipsey. When we see hardly a Sessions pass
at the Old-Bailey, without instances of
wretches hazarding their salvation in the
next world; and, what touches them much
nearer, their ears in this, by perjuring
themselves to bring off their companions:
we ought not to wonder if the same motives should incline them to stay at home,
when for so doing the law has ordain'd
no punishment.

Nothing of all this is pretended to be
true, but it is, what the common story is
not, extremely credible in itself; being no
wise contradictory to our experience of the
actions, passions and interests of mankind; no wise contradictory to the moral
phænomena related of *E. Canning's* character by Mr. *Fielding* and her friends;
and no wise contradictory to certain

physical

phyſical phænomena * of her health, related by Mr. *Dodd*; who, tho' but an indifferent logician, ſeems to be a very careful enquirer into things that relate more
particularly to his own profeſſion.

A month of weeks, as ſhe calls it, being
ſpent in ſome ſuch manner, *ſhe makes a*
ſhift, with her firſt recovery of ſtrength,
to crawl home to her mother's houſe; ill-
colour'd, lean, weak, and in an old gown
and cap (or handkerchief) that did not be-
long to her. The firſt queſtions were, no
doubt, Where have you been? How came
you into this frightful condition? What
is become of your cloaths? Theſe are all
queries that ſhe knew would be put to
her at her return, and it was neceſſary to
have ſome ſort of an anſwer to them; elſe
ſhe muſt, by her ſilence, have paſs'd for
a whore, and have been excluded from
every honeſt family. What could ſhe
anſwer? She could not tell them what we
ſuppoſe to be the truth; and any excuſe,

* Mr. *Dodd*'s phyſical account, page 14.

altho'

altho' it fhould not be believed, was better than none.

She therefore behaved with as much
conduct and difcretion as her unhappy
fituation would allow, and told them a
lie, fo general and void of circumftances,
that fhe had reafon to imagine it could
not be farther traced, and fo her chara-
racter would remain at leaft in a ftate of
doubt; which was gaining a great point
as things ftood with her at the time. Her
lie required no fort of invention, and only
confifted of dry anfwers to the neceffary
queftions that were afked her, viz. *That
fhe had been robb'd of her cloaths and money,
carried fome miles out of town, and confined
with hardly any victuals or drink, in a dark
empty room.* This was the moft particular
defcription fhe could give of her place of
captivity, and was a very blind direction
for thofe who might go in fearch of it.
She probably thought herfelf no lefs fafe
in faying, *that it was fituated near the
Hartford road, as fhe knew by feeing the
Hartford coach go by.* And, indeed, how

C 4   could

could she imagine, that there was any person in the world so sagacious as to be able to tell from the above description, in which of all the houses upon the *Hartford* road she had been a prisoner? But here she was mistaken, and may perhaps some day repent her having been so descriptive. For *either the first night, or early Tuesday morning, one of her friends mentioned the house of mother Wells, she being a most notorious woman ***

The

---

* The reverend author of the letter is supposed here to allude to a case publish'd by *Canning's* friends ten days after her return; which, for the satisfaction of the public, we shall subjoin entire. As likewise a paragraph from the *London Daily Advertiser*, of *Wednesday* the 31*st* of *Jan.* which must have been sent to the printer the very day after she came home; and by which it appears, that her friends had fixed upon *Wells*, and her house, before any of them had been down at *Enfield* to see either, or even before they had been with the sitting alderman.

The CASE of *Elizabeth Canning.*

ELIZABETH CANNING, servant to Mr. *Lyon* in *Aldermanbury*, had leave given her to go and see her uncle and aunt on the first day of *January* last. As she was returning home in the evening of the same day, she was seized by two lusty fellows in *Moorfields*, directly at

the

The innocent countenance and distress-
ed appearance of the girl, joined with her
good

the gates of *Bethlehem* hospital : After they had rifled her
pockets, they took her into the middle walk of the said
fields, where they stripped her of her gown, apron, hat,
&c. She crying out, murder! one of the fellows struck
her on the right temple, which immediately deprived her
of her senses. When she recovered, she found herself in
an open road between the two robbers, who soon convey'd her to a house, in which she saw an old woman and
two young ones. The old woman told her if she would
do as they did, (which was whoring and thieving) she
should want for *nothing* : But upon her refusal, the old
woman cut off her stays, and then forced her up a pair of
stairs, with horrid imprecations, and threatning to cut her
throat if she made the least noise. She was then confined in a *dark room*, and had only about a quartern loaf
in stale and mouldy crusts, and a gallon of water to support her, during the whole time of her confinement, and
a little hay to lie on. On the 29th of *January* she escaped,
by making *a hole in the boards of the window*, about four
o'clock in the afternoon, and came to her mother's house,
about ten at night, in a most miserable condition.

When this unhappy young woman was asked where she
had been, she could give *no other account* than that she had
been confined in a house on the *Hertfordshire* road, which
she knew, by seeing the coachman who drove her mistress
into that country pass by, through a hole of the window.

The house of that notorious woman, well known by
the name of mother *Wells*, between *Enfield Wash* and
Waltham Cross, was immediately suspected ; and from
many circumstances, appears to be the dismal prison of
this unhappy sufferer, whose melancholy situation since

2   her

good character, had from the very first, such an effect upon the good people of the neighbourhood, as to deprive them of all power of examination; so that they never doubted the truth of her ridiculous tale, and were only solicitous to know who

her miraculous escape, as worthy the compassion and charitable contributions of all public-spirited people, and every one who has any regard for the safety of their own children and relations, who are equally liable to the same inhuman and cruel usage, as the beforementioned young person; who since her escape from the house of that monster of a woman, has been in a most deplorable condition; the whole course of nature, having as it were been put out of its usual action; she has, through her uncommon and cruel usage, been deprived of the natural effects of food, nothing having passed through her, since being first hurried away in the manner before-mentioned, but by the art and indefatigable pains of the physician and apothecary who attended her, till the 7th of *February*, when she had an *urinary evacuation*. All these circumstances being duly considered, it is not doubted but a subscription, or contribution will soon be raised, to enable the persons who have undertaken to detect this notorious gang, to prosecute their good intention with the utmost vigour, as such a nest of villains is of the greatest danger to the safety of all his majesty's good subjects.

The truth of the above mentioned facts, we whose names are under written, (inhabitants in and about *Aldermanbury Postern*, who have known the above *Elizabeth Canning*

who were the wretches who had thus
abused her; *and no sooner was the name of*
Wells

Canning from her birth, to have always been a very sober,
honest and industrious girl) *are ready to attest.*

> Francis Roberts.
> Thomas Miles.
> John Marshall.
> Robert Gerrard.
> Jasper Brydon.
> Thomas King.

Cases may be had *gratis*, and donations are taken
in at the *Royal-Exchange Coffee-House* in *Thread-
needle-Street*; at *Lloyd's Coffee-House* in *Lombard-
Street*; at St. *Dunstan's Coffee-house* in *Fleet-Street*;
at Mr. *Say's*, Printer in *Newgate-Street*; and at
Mr. *Francis Roberts's* in *Aldermanbury Postern*, who
is appointed Treasurer for carrying on the pro-
secutions.

Feb. 8th. 1753. *Virtue Hall*, one of the women sworn to
by *Elizabeth Canning*, made a confession before the
worshipful Justice *Fielding*.

Paragraph from the London Daily Advertiser of Wednesday *Jan.* 31.

On Monday night the young woman, who was adver-
tised as left in *Houndsditch* on New Year's day last, about
nine in the evening, came home to her mother, who lives
in *Aldermanbury Postern*, and gave the following extraordinary account of her being forced away and detained.

She had been at *Saltpetre Bank*, near *Rosemary-lane*, to
see

Wells *suggested; though only from their own brains, but they were sure that her house was the scene of all this villany.* Here all doubt and reason took their flight, and left nothing to direct the conduct of those well-meaning *substantial tradesmen,* but passion and enthusiasm.

To confirm their belief of what they no longer doubted, those who knew any thing of *Wells*'s house or its situation, asked her questions concerning it; to which, as she might plainly perceive they were

see her uncle and aunt, who came with her as far as *Houndsditch* in her way home, where she desired them to return. She went from thence into *Moorfields* by *Bethlehem-wall,* as the nigheft way home; there she was met and attacked by two fellows, who pulled off her hat and gown, cut off her apron, then gagged her, and threatened her with bitter imprecations if she cried out to cut her throat. They then forcibly carried her to *Enfield,* to a house kept by one mother *Wells,* near the *Wash* by the ten mile stone, which place they reached about four o'clock in the morning. The fellows left her in that house, and she has not seen them since. *The woman of the house* immediately cut off her stays with her own hands, and with the horridest execrations forced her into a room, where she was kept upon bread and water. She broke her way through a window almoft naked, and in that wretched condition came home. She left several unhappy young women in the house, whose misfortune she has providentially escaped.

asked

afked with a friendly intention, and not with any defign to entrap her, fhe always anfwered, Yes. By which means fhe might poffibly have been furnifhed with fome little knowledge of what fhe was before totally ignorant; and her neighbours, like the boobies who go to aftrologers, were amazed to hear her relate in the afternoon, what their queftions had taught her in the morning. This method of proceeding is not only natural and probable, which is all I require of it, but it likewife appears, by feveral paffages in their accounts, to have been actually their method. *I afked her*, fays Mr. *Scarrat* his depofition at the *Old Bailey*, *if fhe perceived a tanner's houfe near*, fhe faid *fhe believed there was.* I only mention this to fhew how eafy it would be to account for her giving fome particulars relating to a place which fhe never was near, even before fhe was carried down to it, in cafe fhe had given any fuch particulars; which it however does not appear fhe did, by any thing that her friends have

yet

yet publifhed, or that they lay'd before the jury.

However, her compaffionate neighbours thus heated and perfuaded upon their own evidence of the guilt of *Wells*, and the truth of *Canning's* ftory, *upon the Wednefday morning, hurried away the poor creature to repeat it all, before Mr.* Chitty *the fitting alderman, in order to the profecution of* Wells *and her gang; for the defraying of which a fubfcription was fet on foot.*

On Thurfday morning they fet out, Canning, *her mother and other two women, in a coach; and feveral of their neighbours on horfeback, to examine into the affair, and to apprehend the criminals.* And now it will appear how little *Canning* was acquainted with her month's abode. *For although Mr.* Adamfon *was fo good natured as to be there an hour or an hour and a half before the coach arrived; and having feen the room rode back to afk* Canning *feveral queftions concerning it*———which were no doubt afked and anfwered in the manner

manner I have already mentioned. Yet, *notwithstanding all his questions she was so ignorant, that after being seated some time on the dresser of the kitchen into which the room opened, which she has since sworn to be the place of her confinement, yet she never said, That is the room.* But, as Mr. *Adamson* goes on to depose, *after having been carried up* (through a passage) *to examine the house, she said none of the rooms she had seen was the room in which she was confined. Then I asked if there were any other rooms; they said, yes; out of the kitchen (I had before been in it, but did not say so then, because I had a mind to see if she knew it) We had her up into it. She said, This is the same room in which I was, but here is more hay,* &c. *

In all the depositions of the neighbours, besides an extreme eagerness and impatience to communicate their own persuasion, there appears great credulity and simplicity, particularly in this of *Adamson*, who certainly did not mean to instruct

* See the Sessions Paper, p. 114.

Canning

Canning by his returning back to meet her; for if he had meant that, he would not only have afked her *if the room had any hay in it*, or *a chimney in the corner*, but he would have afked her if it did not go out of the kitchen; by which he would have faved her the fatigue of fearching through all the rooms on the other fide of the paffage, and of letting herfelf be ftupidly dragg'd up to the garrets to find the window through which fhe made her efcape, in hopes all the while of feeing *a room with hay in it*, of which fhe had received the hint upon the road; and by that fingle queftion, concerning the door, would have enabled her to point to it as foon as ever fhe entered the kitchen.

In fhort, my Lord, it does not appear diftinctly from any of the evidence produced at the *Old Bailey*, that *Canning* knew any thing at all of this room till fhe was led into it by Mr. *Adamfon*; but that it was then, for the firft time, fhe was furnifhed with the knowledge of

thofe

thofe particulars, which fhe afterwards
put into her depofition, before the juftices,
and the jury, at the trial. Such as *the
bay, the chimney in the corner, the door
out of the kitchen, the faddle, the bafon, and the tobacco mould*; and of every thing but *the jugg*, which, I fuppofe,
is to be found in every houfe upon the
road, and feems to be the only mark, befides *fome plaifter being broken off from the
outfide of the window*, by which Mr. *Adamfon* was directed to chufe this room in preference to the reft.

There has hitherto appeared no contrivance or romantic genius in *Canning* ;
nor has there appeared any occafion for
genius, in order to deceive men who had
fuch an appetite for being deceived.

*The people of the houfe being brought before
her, fhe pitched upon* Mary Squires, *on
account of her fuperior age and uglinefs,
for the miftrefs of the bawdy-houfe, who had
in the miftrefs-like manner fhe related cut off
her ftays* *. *Hereupon fhe and the reft of*

* See the paragraph from the London Daily Advertifer
before inferted.   **D**   Wells's

Wells's *family were put into a cart and car-*
ried in triumph before Juſtice Tyſhmaker,
who, upon the oath of Canning, *and the con-*
curring teſtimony of her friends, committed
Squires *and* Wells *to priſon.*

And here, ſeeing nothing worſe than
human weakneſs and folly in the whole
proceeding, I cannot forbear extending my
tenderneſs to the poor creature whoſe
falſhood I am endeavouring to detect; and
do not ſee, when thus detected, that ſhe
has been guilty of *the blackeſt, moſt premedi-*
tated, and audacious perjury, levelled againſt
the lives of ſeveral innocent perſons, as Mr.
Fielding would repreſent it. There does
not appear any thing *premeditated* or even
voluntary in any of the proceedings of
Canning againſt *Squires* and her companions. We ſee only a lie calculated without the leaſt view beyond that of excuſing
herſelf at a time when her conduct ſtood
greatly in need of an excuſe. All that
followed was entirely owing to the incon-
ſiderate zeal of her friends, which muſt
at firſt have given her infinite comfort, by
relieving

relieving her out of a defperate plunge; and which fhe durft not afterwards check, by not concurring with them in all their inventions, for fear of throwing her affairs back into that fufpicious ftate out of which their warmth had drawn them. So that, by an unavoidable train, fhe was, in a manner, forced to confirm by perjury that lie which fhe had been forced to make. I fay *forced*; for in cafes where an affirmation or oath is offered, manifeftly to acquit the perfon who makes it of fome fuppofed guilt, it can never be reckoned voluntary; and is far from being fo in the eye of the law, which has ever that tender regard to the fouls of men, as not to allow an oath to be adminiftered to thofe, who are fufpected, from a regard to their own lives or charaîters, to be under any fuch temptation of perjuring themfelves.

Upon the 6th of February *Mr.* Fielding, *at the earneft defire of Mr.* Salt *the attorney, undertook to examine into the affair. And next day* Canning *was brought before him, with her information ready drawn up by*

Mr.

Mr. Salt, *to which she swore and put her mark in his presence* *.

But Mr. *Salt*, being a lawyer, knew that the law required two witnesses in order to condemn any person of a capital offence†. *So a warrant was issued to apprehend* Virtue Hall, *who, upon the* 13th, *after some hours of proper management, was brought into*

---

* See Mr. *Fielding*'s pamphlet, page 32, &c.

† Previous to this examination of the 13th, which is all transcribed out of Mr. *Fielding*'s Pamphlet, there appears to have been one on the 8th, which has not fallen under the notice of the Author of this letter, nor mentioned by Mr. *Fielding*, tho' we learn it from the postscript to the case of *Elizabeth Canning* already inserted, and from the following paragraph in the Public Advertiser of Friday the 9th of *February*.

On Wednesday last, at the earnest desire of the Prosecutor, Mr. Justice *Fielding* undertook to examine into the robbery of the girl, who, in the beginning of *January* last, after having been robbed in *Moor-fields*, was carried by two men to a house in *Enfield-Marsh*, where she was stript of her stays, and then confined in a miserable room near a month, with no other sustenance than a quartern loaf and a pitcher of water. On Thursday evening a girl who lived in the house, and who was apprehended by a warrant from the Justice, was brought before him, and was under examination from six till twelve at Night; when, *after many hard struggles and stout denials* of the truth, she *at length confessed* the whole; by which means it is not doubted, but that all the actors of that cruel scene will be brought to the fate they deserve.

Justice

Justice Fielding's *presence, in tears and in a trembling condition. Upon this be endeavoured to comfort her, saying*; Child, you need not be under any fear or apprehension, for if you will tell us the whole truth of the affair, I will give you my word and honour, as far as it is in my power, to protect you. *She answered, she would tell the whole truth. But, altho' the Justice continued to examine her in the kindest manner, she was guilty of so many prevarications and contradictions, that he told her he would examine her no longer, and would leave her to stand or fall by the evidence against her*; *and, at the same time advised Mr.* Salt *to prosecute her as a felon, together with the gypsy woman.* Upon hearing that she was to be prosecuted as a felon, and that her life was to be left to the evidence of persons, who she must think actuated either by the highest degree of madness or wickedness; she thought it was better to trust to Justice *Fielding's* word of honour than their evidence; *and said she would tell the whole truth. So after asking her a few questions, which he says she answered with more appearance of*

D 3   truth

*truth than she had done before, he sent her out
with Mr.* Salt *the attorney, who in two hours
returned with an information in writing, to
which she swore and set her mark before
Justice* Fielding.

That I may not trouble your Lordship with any repetitions, I shall refer
my remarks upon the evidence of *Virtue Hall*, till things come before the
Old Bailey : and shall only say here, that
it was no other than what, bating the
stile, she might have made, without the
help of Mr *Salt*; being only a repetition
of the few circumstances, before related
by *Canning*; and which had been, for a
fortnight preceding, the conversation of
every alehouse within the bills of mor-
tality,

That Justice *Tyshmaker* and Justice *Fielding* might be misled by the simple manner of
Canning is very possible. It is likewise possible, that those who censure them for it at this
time, censure them improperly, by being
acquainted with circumstances, relating to
the affair, unknown to those magistrates,

The

The Event has abundantly juftified their conduct; fince, whether the ftory turns out to be true or falfe, the appearances which are thought fufficient, in a court of juftice fo fair and fo merciful as the *Old Bailey*, to condemn the accufed, muft be more than fufficient to take off any cenfure from a Juftice of peace for the commitment.

Let us therefore proceed to the trial, where your Lordfhip will fee a degree of carelefsnefs, which cannot be accounted for upon any other principle but the force of prepoffeffion; which ferved thofe concerned as an INWARD EVIDENCE of the gypfy's guilt, and made them think any enquiry needlefs, farther than the meer forms of law required.

And yet, perhaps the *Old Bailey* never faw a trial where there were, *prima facie,* more circumftances to render the accufation fufpicious. For befides the numberlefs improbabilities that appear to the dulleft and moft ignorant in the relation of the accufer; there appear, at the firft hearing of the two evidences, *Canning* and

D 4 *Hall,*

Hall, who join in a pretended proof of the principal facts, circumstances that ought to bring their testimony into suspicion, and which it required some pains and questioning to remove.

There is, in the first place, an agreement and a disagreement in their relations, which are of a quite contrary nature to the agreement and disagreement, which are ever known to exist in relations honestly given by different persons concerning the same transaction. For in accounts that are delivered with truth by two different persons concerning the same affair, there will be different circumstances constantly told by the different persons, according as their different memories and apprehensions suggest them to the relators; but when the same facts occur to the relators, there never is, or can be, any thing material in the different manner of relating them.

In the Depositions of *Canning* and *Hall* the direct contrary appears. For *Hall* has not added one original circumstance from her own knowledge,

to

to what had been before related by *Canning*, by which agreement she throws a glaring suspicion of her evidence being a bare repetition of what she had heard from *Canning*: while, on the other hand, she gives positive proofs of her ignorance, by blundering and disagreement, in the manner of relating those circumstances of which *Canning* had given her the hint. Particularly as to the time of bringing in the water-jugg.

The doubts arising from these agreements and disagreements were very natural and obvious, and certainly required much scrutiny. There were accordingly some questions asked, which received answers more tending to increase those doubts than to remove them. Such as, *Did you hear any talk between them* (Wells *and* Squires) *after she* (Canning) *was in the room?* Hall. *They took care I should know but little. In two other answers, she says, she knew nothing of the man who came along with* Squires's *son, and never saw him before or after that night.* It is some-

what

what uncommon for people to be part-
ners of so much deliberate wickedness
with so little knowledge of one another.
*Being asked whether she had ever seen the
cap and ragged bed gown which* Canning
*brought home with her, and said she found
in the grate, she answered, No, she never
did.* Were not these all proofs that her
knowledge went no farther than what
Canning had taught her?

Hall had moreover mentioned a very
curious circumstance in her information
written by Mr. *Salt; that she was the first
that missed* Canning, *which was on the Wednesday, two nights and a complete day, after
she had escaped; and this she repeated at the*
Old Bailey *in these words. I was the first
that missed her, I asked the gipsy woman
once whether the girl was gone, she answered,
what is that to you, you have no business with
it? but durst not go to see if she was gone.
If I had, very like they would have served me
so.* Yet this heap of absurdities passed
without one question to make her explain
what she meant by saying, *she durst not*

go

go to see if she was gone, when she knew
she was gone; or what else it was she
meant by *missing her,* and in what manner she did *miss her.*

It is impossible, my Lord, for two false
witnesses to stand a separate examination
of ten minutes, if it is done with the least
attention; without manifesting, by their
disagreement their ignorance of what they
pretend to know. Never was separate
examination more necessary than in this
case, and yet, so far from employing it,
those questions were not asked which their
actual disagreement seemed to call aloud
for. As for instance, *It was sworn, with
great prolixity, by* Virtue Hall, *that* Fortune Natus, *and his wife had lain constantly in the kitchen for eleven weeks before* Canning's *escape. In another place she
swears that on the* 2d *of* January, *at* 4 *in
the morning, when* Canning *was brought
into the kitchen, where she had her stays cut
off, there were only herself, and the other
three women,* Squires, Wells, *and* Wells's
daughter. Was it not a most natural
question

queſtion to have aſked, where *Fortune Natus* and his wife lay that night, ſince it is plain they were neither in the kitchen nor the hay-loft?

One would imagine it was owing to extreme hurry and ſcarcity of time that thoſe queries were neglected. But that does not appear to have been entirely the caſe; for I have counted in the Seſſions paper at leaſt ſix queſtions put to *Canning* and *Hall* that tend abſolutely to nothing. Such as, aſking at each of them, *How they called the place they put* Canning *into*, &c.

Another great inaccuracy to be obſerv'd in this examination, is; when proper and conducive queſtions were put, ſuffering the witneſs to return anſwers not at all relative to them. As, for inſtance, when the court aſked Mr. *Adamſon, Did any of the people ſeem unwilling to be inſpected?* He anſwered, *Yes, they were unwilling to be ſtop'd.* And then went on with his former narration. But their being unwilling to be *ſtop'd*, was no more an an-

ſwer

fwer to the queftion that was afk'd, than if he had faid, they were unwilling to be hang'd. And yet there the queftion dropt.

But the moft inaccurate part of all the examination, and what tended chiefly to miflead the court, was when the examiners were contented with general and ambiguous anfwers, by which they were made to underftand much more than the witneffes meant; who, it is believed, did not mean to deceive them. This is plainly the cafe in the depofition of *John Wintlebury*, who being afk'd, *Have you heard the evidence fhe* (Canning) *has given in court?*

John Wintlebury. *I have: She gave the fame account, but not fo fully that night as fhe did before the fitting Alderman, on the Wednefday after; but all agrees with what fhe faid here.*

R. Scarrat likewife anfwers to the fame queftion. *I alfo heard E. Canning examined before the fitting Alderman. She gave the fame account fhe has done here.*

Thefe two witneffes feemed to fay fomething very fatisfactory to the court; but,

if

if they had been made to explain themfelves, it would have all vanifhed away.
For they, by this general anfwer, meant
no more than that what fhe faid before
Mr. *Chitty*, the fitting Alderman, did not
contradict her evidence before the jury;
but the court certainly underftood by it,
that fhe had given as full an evidence
then, with regard to particulars, as fhe
did at the *Old-Bailey*. This ambiguity,
which I dare fay helped very much to
forward the belief of *Canning*'s ftory, and
the Gipfy's condemnation, would have
been eafily removed, by afking the following queftions.

Did *Canning*, when before the fitting
Alderman, give any particular defcription
of the room in which fhe had been
confined?

Did fhe mention any hay being in it?

Did fhe defcribe a chimney in the corner?

Did fhe mention any other furniture befides the jugg?

Did fhe mention the faddle and the
bafon?

Did

Did she mention the tobacco mould, which, being of so particular a nature, would have been sufficient in itself to have proved her having been in the room, where it was afterwards found?

Did she describe the stairs, as being on the inside of the door, and the door opening into the kitchen?

Did she say, the woman that cut her stays took the knife out of the drawer of the dresser?

If these questions had been asked, there is no reason to believe but that they would have been all answer'd in the negative, altho' the witnesses seem'd, in their general answer, to affirm them all, by mistaking the intention of the court. It would have then appear'd, that *Canning*, in swearing to all these particularities, in court, and before the justices, had sworn to what she did not know till the day after she was before the sitting Alderman; and that, consequently, her story, if it was not proved false, was, at least, proved to have no support from external circum-

I   stances;

ftances; and that it refted barely upon her
own oath and that of *Virtue Hall*, the
nature of which has been already explained. But the queftions, as abuve, not being
afked, the fact was thought to be prov'd,
and the poor gipfy condemn'd to death.

The *evidence of fact*, as Mr. *Fielding*
very juftly obferves, *is alone fafely to be*
depended on, as it is alone incapable of a lie.
And yet, it was fo far from being regard-
ed in this trial, that, tho' it never appear'd ftronger upon any occafion than
againft *Canning*, the poor wretch *Squires*
would have been long ago hang'd; if that
fentence,. which no *evidentia rei* were capable of refpiting, had not been refpited by
the oath of an acknowledged perjurer:
Of fuch weight is perfonal authority, in
oppofition to reafon and experience. Such
is the credit of oaths, in this land of
perjury.

Thus, my Lord, I have run over, in
as few words as I could, the principal
circumftances that mark the incredibility
of *Canning*'s relation; the various fteps
by

2

by which it acquir'd credit; and some of
the moſt obvious omiſſions, which prevent-
ed thoſe falſhoods and miſtakes from being
detected, at the trial. And, I muſt own,
that, altho' I am not at all fond of writing,
I was glad that your curioſity furniſhed
me with an opportunity of writing upon
this ſubject to your Lordſhip, to whom I
am bound by many ties of duty and affection. For this is not barely an enquiry concerning a pair of old ſtays, or
the bad diet of a ſervant wench; nor
about the life of an old gipſy (tho' no man
ought to think himſelf too great to intereſt
himſelf in the diſtreſſes of the meaneſt)
but it is an enquiry of a much more intereſting kind: no leſs than *an enquiry
into the nature of moral evidence,* the
axis upon which all human affairs turn,
and of which the true knowledge is of the
greateſt uſe to perſons of all ranks; and
is doubly neceſſary to one of your Lordſhip's high ſtation; as you not only require
it for the conduct of your own peculiar concerns, but muſt make uſe of it likewiſe in

E   dif-

difposing of the property, and fometimes of the lives of your fellow fubjects, as a member of that high court of judicature, in which your noble birth will foon entitle you to a feat. It is for this reafon, I have been glad of an opening to communicate to you what my years and experience have furnished me with upon this fubject; and wifh, that fome more able pen would undertake the fame tafk for the publick; which, if I may guefs by the foregoing tranfaction, ftands greatly in need of fome inftruction.

And indeed, by the free and happy con-ftitution of our country, it fo happens, that the loweft man in it may be call'd upon, as a jury-man, to decide in mat-ters that immediately concern the lives and goods of his fellow fubjects; where an ignorance in examining and weighing the evidence brought before him, may be attended with very fatal confequences to others, and of future uneafinefs of mind to himfelf; as might have happen'd to the twelve well meaning men who condemn'd

Squires;

Squires; had it not pleafed God, by un-
expected means, to prevent the execution
of the fentence.

In fhort, my Lord, the *jurymen*, except in thofe cafes, which come before the
court of Chancery, and the houfe of Peers,
are the fole JUDGES of the lives and properties of Englifhmen. That I may fhew
you this in the ftrongeft light, it will not
be improper to give you a detail of
thofe perfonages that compofe an Englifh
court of juftice; fuch as they are in FACT,
and ftripp'd of the common *words* in
which they are difguifed.

There is firft the PROSECUTOR and
CRIMINAL, or, as they are called in cafes
of *meum & tuum*, the PLAINTIFF and DE-
FENDANT. Next there are the fworn
JUDGES of the trial or caufe, who are called the *jury*, compofed of difinterefted men
of unblemifhed characters. All the reft of
the perfonages, though called by various
names, are only, *in fact*, different kinds
of EVIDENCES.

First

First there are those who are called in common language the EVIDENCES or WITNESSES; who are supposed to be disinterested, and relate, upon oath, what they know, concerning the relation which the criminal, or defendant, bears to the fact of which he is accused.

The second sort of EVIDENCE go by the name of *council*, who are to inform the aforesaid JUDGES or *jury-men*, what they know, concerning the relation in which the fact stands to the laws of the land. But this sort of EVIDENCE differs extremely from the first, inasmuch as they do not deliver their evidence upon oath, and so far from being disinterested, are professedly SUBORNED, or as they term it *fee'd*. Their veracity has therefore no sort of stress laid upon it, which gives rise to

A third sort of EVIDENCE, commonly called *the judge*, not from any power of deciding, which is lodged solely in those twelve JUDGES, whose verdict is definitive and uncontroulable; but from his sitting in the same high place where *actual judges*

judges fit in other countries. And is perhaps for this reason sometimes called *the bench*. This fort of EVIDENCE is like the second, well learned in the law, but differs from them, in having taken an oath to be honeft, and is, by his fituation in life, out of fufpicion of being fuborned. His office is, to give true evidence concerning the relation which the laws of the land bear to the crime of which the party is accufed; and to prevent the FEE'D EVIDENCES from deceiving the twelve JUDGES, by laying falfhoods concerning thofe laws before them. An Englifh *judge* may be juftly confidered as a living *Corpus juris*, publifhed by authority, for the ufe of the unlearned; which needs no index, but opens of itfelf, wherever it is neceffary, and is, upon every occafion, its own commentary.

I have indeed heard from fome of the gentlemen of *Weftminfter-hall*, that jurymen are judges of *fact*, but not of *law*. A diftinction, fuch as one often meets

E 3 with

with amongst the learned, without a difference; since there is no question can
arise concerning law, or concerning any
thing else that has a real existence, which
is not a question concerning matter of
fact: so that, if it is the office of jurymen to be judges of fact, their office is to
judge of every thing which is the proper
object of the human understanding. This
is not only plain to abstract reasoners, but
is obvious to the common sense of mankind; and is, notwithstanding the learning of the learned, the actual practice of
our courts of justice, where jurymen every day give a peremptory decision concerning the causes that come before them;
and acquit or condemn, without thinking
themselves obliged to account for the
grounds of their determination.

This being fairly the case, it extremely
behoveth every man who may be called
upon to sit in judgment, that is every
Englishman, to make himself well acquainted with the nature of evidence; how

I

to weigh one thing against another, and to distinguish the true from the counterfeit. For my own part, altho' I shall always look upon a trial by juries as the great bulwark of our political liberty; yet, in the present state of ignorance, credulity, and irregular method of enquiry, I should be extremely fearful of my life and character, if I were accused of a capital offence; and should, by no means, think my innocence a sufficient protection.

It was formerly ordained, for the security of the accused person, that there should be the oaths of two credible witnesses against him, before he could be legally condemned. From hence, by a most absurd conclusion, it is presumed that the oaths of two persons are a sufficient proof of the truth of any fact, be it ever so unaccountable; so that if a man is accused of murdering another upon a certain day, and then by way of concealment, eating him up, at a meal, (a fact uncapable of proof from any human testimo-

ny,

ny, becaufe it will always be more likely that any number of men fhould be deceived, or have an intention of deceiving, than that fuch a thing fhould have really happened) yet if this is fworn to, by two perfons of unimpeached charaêters, the jury is bound in confcience to bring him in guilty; and nothing can fave him, unlefs, by fair or foul means, he can bring two other perfons from *Plymouth* or *Coventry*, to fwear an *alibi*, and that they fmoaked a pipe, or played at whift with him upon the Day mentioned.

To prevent this abfurd method of proceeding, and the cruel confequences attending it, it is incumbent on the learned, who know the rules of probability, to divulge all thofe rules to the public, and efpecially to explain more fully, and enforce the principle with which I fet out in the beginning of this letter, *that no evidence is to be received in proof of any faêt, unlefs its weight is ftriêtly conformable to the improbability of the faêt it means to prove.*

But

But no perſon who is in the leaſt acquainted with the preſent or paſt times,
or has made any obſervations on men and
manners, will urge: That it is a very unu-
ſual thing to find human teſtimony falſe,
or that it is very improbable it ſhould
turn out to be ſo; therefore human teſtimony is never to be urged in ſupport of
any fact that is, beyond a certain degree,
improbable,

It is the want of having been acquainted with this, which has occaſion'd thoſe, who
have reaſon'd in favour of *Canning*, to fall
into an error. They have thought it ſufficient, if they could find poſſible means of
accounting for ſome one, out of the great
number of improbabilities related by her;
or of finding evidence, of weight ſufficient to over-balance it. But they have
never conſider'd, that when the number of
thoſe improbabilities is very great, their
accumulation amounts to ſomething ſo
near to an impoſſibility, that it may
juſtly, in common language, be ſo called.

A man

A man who tells us, that he faw twenty
aces thrown at one throw, by twenty fair
dice, may perhaps, if his character is
good, gain credit; but if he tells us, that
he faw the fame throw repeated twenty
times running, there is no man of fenfe,
who will fcruple to pronounce, that there
was falfhood, either in the dice, or the
ftory teller.

Thus, my Lord, I have run through
all, that at prefent occurs to me worth
mentioning on this affair; and I dare
fay, have intruded much longer on your
patience, than you expected. I can make
no other apology for it, but reminding
you, that it is always dangerous to fet an
old man a tattling: and, as *George Dandin*
fays, *vous l'avez voulu*; fo you muft take
the confequence.

Every thing is now fettled with regard
to my nephew's commiffion, in which I
have received great affiftance from Lord
————. I intend, on *Wednefday*, to ac-
company him as far as St. *Albans*, on
his

his way to *Holy-Head*, and ſhall next day ſet out for your Lordſhip and my charge, from which I have been too long abſent, and am, with the greateſt reſpect and affection,

My LORD,

Your Lordſhip's, &c.

LONDON, *May* 15, 1753.

A N

E S S A Y

ON THE

NATURALIZATION

OF

FOREIGNERS.

THE SECOND EDITION.

Visam Britannos hospitibus feros.   HOR.

Νηπιοι ϰδ᾽ ισασιν ὁσῳ πλεον ἡμισυ παντος. HESIOD.

L O N D O N:

Printed in the Year M DCC LXII.

E S S A Y

Naturalization of Foreigners.

AMONGST the various productions
with which the paſt time has enlighten-
ed the preſent, there are none which may be
more ſafely relied on than thoſe anonymous
pieces which go by the name of Proverbs. We
find that nonſenſe of every kind is received with
applauſe, when it happens to drop from what
is called *a great Name*; and that it is ſometimes,
on the ſame account, tranſmitted from age to
age, like the toe-nail-parings of St. NICOLAS,
with religious veneration and aſtoniſhment. But
thoſe proverbial maxims, not being able to tell
who was their ſire, and pretending to no rank,
but what their own merit procures them, could
not poſſibly have ſupported their credit ſo long
in the world, if experience, from which they
originally ſprung, had not been conſtantly ready
to atteſt their veracity. They are the true philoſophy of the vulgar, and are extremely uſeful

B   in

in the conduct of private life. In this respect, THE VOICE OF THE PEOPLE may be said to be THE VOICE OF GOD; but in no other: for, if ever that saying is meant to recommend the opinions of the vulgar in matters of more general consequence, there are few common sayings so untrue. The business of the bulk of mankind is not to think, but to act, each in his own little sphere, and for his own little purposes; and this he may do, very completely, without much reflection, by the force of habit alone: leaving the conduct of the whole to the few of a more extended way of thinking; or to the great Conductor of the universe, according to that more than vulgar proverb, EVERY MAN FOR HIMSELF, AND GOD FOR US ALL.

A HABERDASHER of small ware, for instance, if he happens to be but one degree above an idiot, knows, by the help of those maxims, how to manage his own peculiar business to the encrease of his stock, and the security of his family, better than if he were directed by the best philosopher of them all. He knows that he is to buy cheap and to sell dear, and, for that purpose, to keep the trade in as few hands as possible, and to burn, sink, and destroy all those who take upon them to haberdash, without being *free of the company*; knowing, that though THE MORE THE MERRIER, yet, THE FEWER THE BETTER CHEAR. He likewise knows, that A PENNY SAV'D IS A PENNY GOT,

GOT, and consequently, that in his family, there is need of certain *sumptuary laws*, to prevent himself from going too often to the Punch-house, or Sadler's-Wells; and his wife from wearing more silk gowns than the nature of gossipping absolutely requires. To preserve the grandeur and dignity of his family he says, BETTER AN EMPTY HOUSE THAN A BAD TENANT; and from thence concludes, that it is better his daughters should go virgins into the other world,

With all their imperfections on their heads,

than that they should slip away to May-fair-Chapel with foot soldiers, or hackney-coachmen, and bring forth a numerous progeny to light lamps, or cry mackarel about the streets.

Certainly nothing can be more just than these maxims; and a steady adherence to them must, in time, procure him his desired ten thousand; make him a very respectable man in his ward, perhaps an alderman; and Miss BIDDY and Miss SUKEY, besides living in ease and affluence, may come, at the age of fifty, to be look'd upon as *very genteel sort of girls*, and to be visited by Sir HUMPHREY GUTTLE's lady, and the best ladies in the lane.

But when my haberdashing friend has brought his wisdom so far, there let him stop. Let him not, in the pride of his success, fancy he has *a head*, and that he could make the state richer, happier, and more respectable, by the same

means

means which he has employed to raife his own family: for the moment he applies his maxims to any thing out of the walls of his own houfe and fhop, that moment he launches out into the boundlefs ocean of abfurdity. A ftate, and a fingle family in that ftate, do not differ in magnitude only, as is generally imagined, but are very different in their nature, and muft be fometimes conducted and improved by means (in all appearance, at leaft) directly oppofite. This general propofition, and the bad confequences which have refulted to the public for want of a due attention to it, may, perhaps, be the fubject of our future enquiry. At prefent I fhall only take notice of one particular vulgarity, a confequence of one of the foregoing maxims, which has always prevailed, more or lefs, in this Ifland; tho', I think, of late, with more than ordinary noife: and that is, the complaint that foreigners are employed in England, in great numbers, to the prejudice of the natives. This complaint is not entirely confined to the waiftcoated populace, tho' it, no doubt, began there; but has afcended from them to others who wear coats, nay, laced waiftcoats; from thefe to hackney writers, whofe fentiments have been fometimes drivel'd out in fenatorial fpeeches.

An attempt, indeed, has been made to difcountenance this narrow and injudicioufly felfifh fpirit, by bringing in a bill, giving the rights of Britifh fubjects to all thofe, wherever they may
hap-

happen to be born, who are willing to make a part of our happy conftitution in church and ftate. *But it pleafed not the million*, and was thrown out, for reafons which would be very entertaining, if they could be all collected and compared together. " What," fays a fox-hunting 'fquire, " would you let in an inundation of beggars upon us, without art or induftry, to become an additional burden to the poor's-rate, already too heavy for our fhoulders?" " There fpoke the tongue of an angel," fays his taylor : " Good, your honour, ftand by Old England, and don't encourage any more of thofe vagabonds to come over ; for we have but too many of them already to take the bread out of our mouths." How is it poffible to reconcile thefe two opinions concerning foreigners, fo oppofite, and yet fo common in the mouths of thofe who are willing to exclude them? One reprefents them as fo many idle drones, that fatten upon the labours of the reft: the other, as fo intolerably bufy as not to fuffer any body to be employed but themfelves.

If experience may be allowed to decide in this matter, the taylor's reafon will alone be found to have even the appearance of foundation ; and hence arife moft of the complaints of the vulgar. It is certainly true that foreigners are apt to take the bread out of fome mouths. But out of whofe mouths? The mouths of the proud, the idle, the ignorant, and the debauched. And are

we,

we, for the clamours of such, to deprive the nation of the great advantage which must accrue to it, from the accession of so many skilful and industrious hands, which the hopes of living better than in their own countries, daily brings over to us? Neither are those complaints, mean as they are, in general, well founded. For those very grumblers owe part of the little bread they enjoy, to the general wealth, which the industry of foreigners has brought into their country. I should be glad to know what sort of a figure this island would make, if it were to refund to the continent all those whose names shew them to be of foreign extraction. Let it refund their own to the Saxons, Danes, Normans, French and Germans, and, I believe, there are few of the rest who would choose to remain in it. They all, however, join in the common cry against new comers; and yet, it is certain, that the ancestors of one half of them were once strangers; and there is as little doubt that the posterity of those, who are now strangers, will, in a very short time, call themselves Englishmen; and may perhaps, like the rest, fling dirt at their forefathers, by shutting the door, in an opprobrious manner, upon others who have an equal title to be admitted. He is an Englishman, and he alone, who contributes to enrich and defend England; and he who does

not,

not, is an Alien, if he merit not a worſe appellation. The time may come,

Εσσεῖαι ἡμαϱ ὁτ᾽ αν ποτ᾽ ολωλῃ Ιλιος ιϱη,
Και Πϱιαμος, και λαος εὔμμελιω Πϱιαμοιο,

the time may come, when the tide of proſperity
may ebb, which ſtill flows into this happy iſland,
and may not only carry back many of the foreigners it now brings, but many of the natives
along with them. Would they who grumble
at the encouragement now given to foreigners
in England, be glad to hear that Engliſhmen
are better fed abroad than at home, and that
half the ſhops in Paris were occupied by them?
They would, undoubtedly, grieve at the news
inſtead of rejoicing, which they ought naturally
to do if their preſent complaints had any thing
rational in their foundation.

In the year 1744, this excluſive, this perſe-
cuting, this corporation ſpirit ſeized with great
violence upon the Engliſh footmen, and gave a
beginning to a ſort of *bellum ſervile*, in the very
heart of this great metropolis. A ſelect com-
mittee of thoſe gentlemen advertiſed a rendez-
vous in the news papers, to be held at *Hickford*'s
great room, *in order to concert ways and means
to oblige their maſters to turn away all their foreign ſervants*. But this combination, ſo abominable, if it could have been at all ſupported,
became next day extremely ridiculous, by the
vigilance and courage of Juſtice DE VEIL; who,

for

for the virtues, civil and military, which he exerted upon this occasion, received, from his majesty's hand, the honour of knighthood.

But, altho' this gallant and useful service was *pleasing to the superior powers, the cause of the vanquished did not cease to be dear to many* Cato's, male and female, who thought that no demand could be more reasonable than for British-born subjects to enjoy a monopoly of vails and laziness, by which their vails and laziness would come to be greatly encreased; and thereby that proper equality be preserved betwixt master and servant, so essential to the freedom and independency of the British constitution.

To shew how ill these good people reason in what relates to the general interest of their country, let us suppose a practice established the very reverse of what they approve, and, that the fashion of keeping foreign servants were carried so high as totally to exclude the natives from wearing liveries. It is demonstrable that such a fashion, however foolish in its motives, would be attended with the greatest advantages to Britain. For, first, we should have much less chance of cabals and combinations from men, who, being brought from all corners of Europe, and incapable of combining under any title but the most odious and unpopular, could have no prospect of relief from a corporation-fund, after a forfeiture of their services and characters. Secondly, we should be much better served by those

those who had received the early habits of sub-
mission, in countries where subordination is better established, than by those who think they
degrade and debase the Briton, if they conde-
scend to do above one third of the work for
which they are paid.

These, indeed, are only private considera-
tions, whose truth cannot be absolutely ascertained without a greater number of experiments
than any body will ever take the pains of collecting. But tho' the advantage or disadvantage
to private families, arising from such a fashion,
should be still a subject of dispute, the advantage, with regard to the public, will bear no
controversy.

For the high wages and vails would draw
young men enough from all quarters of the
world, to fill ever so many liveries; and, when
one race of those men extinguished, the laws,
which fashion and conveniency have established,
requiring celibacy from footmen almost as much
as from dominicans, they would be recruited
fresh and fresh every day by new comers from
abroad. Let those who *talk* of their country,
for once *think* what benefits would arise to it
from such an extraneous aid. Let them think
how many thousands of able-bodied young men
would be preserved to the farms and manufac-
turing towns, who now come in shoals to London, upon the prospect of living there in a lux-
urious and lazy manner. Let them think how
many

many would be spared to encrease the national riches by commerce, and the national glory by arms, who now, for want of worse hands, loiter away their youth in the halls and kitchens of the rich. These patriots surely are not afraid that the price of labour will become so low to the farmer, that he will be enabled to pay too much rent, and export too much corn to foreign markets. They cannot be afraid that the price of labour will become so low to the manufacturer, that he will be enabled to export his broad cloth too cheap to Turkey, and by that means supplant the French, who have almost entirely deprived us of that branch of commerce. But if these are not their fears, it is hard to say what they are afraid of, since these are two of the most obvious consequences attending the reception of foreign servants. I know there are some who pretend that there is danger of the foreigners, settled amongst us, joining in any hostile Invasion to conquer or distress this island. But this fear, real or pretended, is ill supported by any kind of reasoning, and least of all by experience; which, in all our intestine commotions, kept these foreigners ever free from any suspicion of treason; and has discovered an uncommon zeal for the defence of the government in such of them as are protestants, for whom alone any public encouragement was intended.

And what, after all, is this *public encouragement*, which was proposed by a general bill of

7

natu-

naturalization ? Nothing but the removal of the *public difcouragements*, which the ignorance of former times had, by exprefs laws, laid upon foreigners, to this nation's detriment as well as theirs. It was only meant to permit them to come over, ready trained, to do our work, to man our fleets, to pay our taxes, and to maintain our poor. " No," fays a leading man in the veftry, " that is not all; they will expect " likewife to be maintained in their turn, when- " ever any of them happens to be unfitted for " labour, by ficknefs or old age." This is a very common objection, and, perhaps, we may find it full of fenfe and equity; efpecially, when we confider that the parifh could not be fuppofed to have the pleafure of feeding, cloathing, and teaching them in their infancy.

To be ferious, there is no danger of any infirm people leaving their native countries, upon the hopes of getting a fhare of the pitiful pittance, which is left by the parifh officers, for the maintenance of the public poor. Thofe who are found to leave their native countries, in order to feek their fortunes in diftant climates, are not the old, the maimed, the fick, and the diftreft; but the young, the healthy, the vigorous and the vain; thofe who have, or fancy they have, talents, which will give them a fuperiority over the inhabitants of thofe countries to which they chufe to migrate. The natives of every country have great advantages in
bufinef;

buſineſs over ſtrangers, ariſing from that circumſtance alone of their nativity. It is a great point
in buſineſs to ſet out with the knowledge of the
language and cuſtoms of the country, to enjoy
the aſſiſtance of relations and ſchool-fellows; and
to have cuſtomers tranſmitted by habit from
maſter to apprentice; in all which reſpeɛts the
diſadvantages of foreigners can only be compen-
ſated by ſuperior ſkill and induſtry.

But, ſay their oppoſers, were the foreigners
to recommend themſelves only by their ſuperior
ſkill and induſtry, we ſhould not dare to complain; but they make themſelves acceptable to
the rich and the giddy, by oddities and artifices,
altogether unconnected with their callings. For
inſtance, ſay they, we ſhall have an artiſt, who,
though inferior in talents to ſeveral of our own
countrymen, ſhall carry away the vogue from
them all, by wearing a long beard, and looking like a Turk, when there are twenty perſons
ready to make oath, that he is neither better
nor worſe than a chriſtian. And is this a cauſe
of complaint? One would think that Engliſhmen had no beards, or that there was a law here,
as in Ruſſia, to prohibit the growth of them.
The gentleman does not, as I have been informed, pretend to any excluſive patent for theſe his
accoutrements; and if he has diſcovered, that
by ſubmitting to eat his bread with the ſweat of
his muſtachio's, he ſhall earn better bread than
would otherwiſe come to his ſhare, it would be
foolishly

foolifhly difputing *Tafles*, to find fault with the
proceeding.

In fhort, be that as it will, it ought to have
no place in a queftion betwixt Englifh and Foreigners. Quackery and affectation are the
growth of every climate ; and of our own dear
country as much, at leaft, as of any other under the fun. Long before this hairy phænome-
non landed at Dover, that force of Englifh genius, which laid open to Sir ISAAC NEWTON
the laws of attraction, had difcovered to the famous TIDDIDOL that there was a virtue in par-
ticles of filver-lace, artfully difpofed upon an old
hat and coat, that would greatly accelerate the
circulation of gingerbread. The effects of this
talifmanic contrivance are well known ; the
caufe and manner of its operation are not fo obvious. All we know is, that it acts upon thofe
who come within its vortex; but in what ratio,
whether according to the cube, or the fquare of
the diftance, is yet undetermined by philofophers. For my own part, being totally ignorant
of geometry, and at the fame time not fuperfti-
tious enough to believe, that there is any fympa-
thy fubfifting betwixt the filver upon TIDDI-
DOL's hat, and the copper in the pockets of his
cuftomers ; I am inclined to think, that it affects
their underftandings only, and that the procefs
is entirely of a logical nature. The aftonifhed
people fee, that thofe bits of filver-lace, make
TIDDIDOL an extraordinary fine gingerbread
baker ;

baker; and then conclude that an extraordinary fine gingerbread baker muſt bake extraordinary fine gingerbread. I am not ſure, that this is extraordinary ſound reaſoning, but I am ſure, from many years obſervation, that it is as con-cluſive in favour of artiſts, born upon the banks of the Thames, as of thoſe who come from the Rhone or the Tiber.

Before I take leave of this ſubject, it may not be amiſs to make a remark or two upon the word *Alien*, when applied to perſons reſident in England. He is, it ſeems, an alien, and by law ſubject to various diſcouragements, *who is born of foreign parents, in a foreign country*. A law-deſcription altogether arbitrary, and no bet-ter grounded on the real nature of citizenſhip, than if it declared thoſe to be aliens, who were born with ſuch coloured eyes, or in ſuch a ſea-ſon. One way to be ſenſible of this, is to ex-amine the two diſqualifications ſeparately, and to aſk: Is it being born in a diſtant country which unfits a man from being a freeman of England? No; for the ſons of Engliſhmen born abroad are all Engliſh. Is it then being born of foreign parents? No; for the ſons of foreigners, if born in England, are acknow-ledged to be Engliſh. It is inconceivable, why neither of thoſe circumſtances of birth, taken ſingly, ſhould tend to diſqualify the perſon ſo born, and yet, that by a ſtrange ſort of arith-metic,

metic, the addition of thofe two nothings, fhould produce a fomething fo difadvantageous.

In whatever light we view this diftinction, I am confident it will be found to owe its deriva- tion entirely to the municipal laws of this ifland ; and, confequently, a repeal of thofe laws, by a general act of Naturalization, would entirely remove it; and then every man, refiding in Eng- land, would be an Englifhman to all intents and purpofes. So that to oppofe fuch an act, is, in other words, to affent to laws, by which many thoufands of Englifhmen are excluded from this country, and from partaking of benefits, which, by the bare participation, they would propor- tionably encreafe, and be equally entitled to with the reft. To talk of a foreigner, natura- lized by refidence, as a foreigner, is as great an abufe of language, as to talk of melted ice, as ice. For as the latter becomes water by melting, lofing all the properties of ice ; fo the other be- comes an Englifhman, ipfo facto, by the in- corporation : and any reafonings, drawn from his former ftate, can only ferve to miflead the fhallow and unthinking.

Let us therefore lay afide all fuch unnatural diftinctions, that divert our attention from thofe, which it is ever deftructive to overlook. Let us be careful to diftinguifh honeft men from knaves, labourers from drones, and ingenious men from coxcombs : Let us punifh crimes, ftarve lazinefs, and ridicule falfe pretence, whe- ther the culprit be Trojan or Tyrian : But let

us

us not sacrifice useful realities to unmeaning
words; nor submit the learning and experience
of the present age, to the narrow-hearted whims
of our ignorant and savage progenitors.

A

DIALOGUE

ON

TASTE.

Ουδεν εν ανθροποισι διακριδον εστι νοημα,
 Αλλ' ὁ συ θαυμαζοις τουθ' ετεροιτι γελως.   Lucian.

Mille hominum species, et rerum discolor usus:
Velle suum cuique est, nec voto vivitur uno.   Persius.

The SECOND EDITION.

LONDON:

Printed in the Year MDCCLXII.

A

DIALOGUE

ON

TASTE.

Lord MODISH's Country-Seat.

Lord and Lady MODISH, Lady HARRIOT, and Colonel FREEMAN.

Lord MODISH.

AND so you prefer HUDIBRAS to VIRGIL?

Col. FREEMAN.

I do indeed, my Lord.

Lord MODISH.

But why, my noble Colonel?

Col. FREEMAN.

Because he gives me most pleasure.

A 2

Lord MODISH.

Then allow me to tell you, George, you are with all your reading an abſolute Goth, and have no manner of taſte.

Col. FREEMAN.

So you told me laſt night, my Lord, when I preferred Canary to Champaign.

Lord MODISH.

No doubt; for that was juſt ſuch another inſtance of your Gothicneſs.

Col. FREEMAN.

I agree with your Lordſhip that the caſes are very parallel, and for that reaſon I mention your laſt night's obſervation. The word *taſte* originally belongs to the palate, and it is not amiſs to have that always in view, when we ſuſpect a miſapplication of it in the way of metaphor. It is by taſte, no doubt, that we are able to diſtinguiſh ſalt from ſugar, and muſtard from applepie; its proper office being upon all ſuch occaſions to inform us what is what. But allow me to aſk your Lordſhip, why you ſaid I had no taſte in wine, when it was plain, by my preference of one of the bottles, that I could very well diſtinguiſh it from the reſt.

Lord

Lord MODISH.

You certainly now affect to misunderstand me. By saying you had no taste, I did not mean that you was not capable of distinguishing; but, according to the usual application of the phrase, that you had a bad taste, and preferred the worst.

Col. FREEMAN.

This is, my Lord, an application of the word *taste*, that, however usual, somewhat deviates from its original and proper sense. For, according to that, good taste can signify no more than a greater than ordinary accuracy in determining, in certain cases, that two distinct things are of the same or of different kinds, and when of different kinds in assigning the proper name to each. Take a man so endowed into your cellar, and without seeing the labels, he will tell you not only that this hogshead is Port and that Claret, but amongst the Clarets that this is of such a growth and such a year, that of such another. I am very sensible that your Lordship's application of the phrase is nevertheless usual : but if all the phrases that convey no distinct and invariable meaning were banished out of the world, we should be deprived, among the rest, of a great many that are very usual and fashionable. But, *a propos* of our last night's liquor, did you mean by the worst the least whole-

wholefome? If fo, I am afraid my tafte can hardly be defended.

Lord MODISH.

No, faith; I believe the Champaign is the worft of the two in that refpect. No; I meant that which had the worft flavour.

Col. FREEMAN.

Then I fuppofe you think me infincere in my declaration of liking Canary.

Lord MODISH.

I have known you too long, George, to lay infincerity to your charge. No; I make no doubt of your having really a very bad tafte in your potations.

Col. FREEMAN.

You mean, then, I dare fay, that it is not your tafte.

Lord MODISH.

No; nor of any of your acquaintance, I'll be fworn.

Col. FREEMAN.

So then the goodnefs or badnefs of one's tafte is to be determined by the tafte of the majority.

Lord MODISH.

Certainly; and were it otherwife what con-fufion muft enfue? for when men are to drink jovially together, it is highly reafonable that the

few

few should yield in the choice of the liquor to the many.

Col. FREEMAN.

My Lord, I will allow your consequence: But what necessity is there for this society in drink, by which the conformity becomes necessary? When soldiers are to attack the enemy, such an union must be absolutely necessary; else one platoon might retire whilst another advanced. It is no less necessary where more pacific people are met to dance country-dances; else the man might be footing corners, whilst his partner was figuring in. Unless all fight and dance with one accord, the purposes of fighting and dancing would be entirely frustrated. But there is nothing in the nature of drinking, that hinders it from being performed as effectually, and to as good purpose, by a single person, as by one that has thirty legions at his back. When you can make it appear that a man ought to take physic because his friend his sick, or to drink because he is dry, it may then appear reasonable in him to drink of a particular kind of liquor because his companions happen to be pleased with the flavour of it: an extraordinary stretch of complaisance, from which no person seems to reap any advantage. For my own part, I profess myself an entire friend to toleration and liberty of conscience, and think it little better than popery and the inquisition to compel any man to swallow what

A 4   goes

goes againſt his ſtomach, on pretence of preſerving unity in public drinking.

Lord MODISH.

Thou art an odd fellow, George, that is certain.

Col. FREEMAN.

I am indeed, my Lord; for I always deliver my own ſentiments, and in my own words.

Lord MODISH.

So then you reckon religion and drinking to be of the ſame nature. I think I have known you ſometimes more lucky in your compariſons.

Col. FREEMAN.

I don't pretend, my Lord, that the parallel will hold in every reſpect; but with regard to the ſubject of our preſent converſation they are certainly very much akin: being both matters of private concern and advantage only; and, of courſe, the objects only of taſte or private opinion. But when I ſpeak of religion, I would be underſtood of what is ſpeculative and ritual, and not at all of the moral duties: So when I ſpeak of drinking, I mean drinking for pleaſure, without taking any of its medicinal effects into conſideration; for as by theſe ſociety may be affected, they are very properly the objects of general concern and enquiry.

Lord

Lord MODISH.

Then you don't allow the moral duties to be the objects of taste. My Lord Shaftesbury is of a very different opinion.

Col. FREEMAN.

That may be; but his Lordship stands not for divine authority with me. I know, my Lord, that there has been much unfortunate pains employed, by many authors from Plato down to Sir Harry Beaumont, in order to confound the objects of judgment with those of taste and feeling; than which nothing can be more vulgar and unphilosophical.

Lord MODISH.

I fancy it is not an easy matter to separate them; and, as I know you have turned your mind pretty much to such enquiries, I should be glad to know what touchstone you recommend for that purpose.

Col. FREEMAN.

It does not appear to me so difficult as it seems to those refined philosophers; and thus I distinguish them. Whatever has a rule or standard to which it may be referred, and is capable of comparison, is not the object of taste, but of reason and judgment. On the other hand, the proper objects of taste, or feeling, are such as are relative to the person only who is actuated by them, who is the sole judge whether those feelings be agreeable, or otherwise; and
being

being informed of this simple fact from himself,
no farther consequence can be drawn from it,
neither does it admit of any dispute. Thus when
a man tells me that venison eats better with currant than with gravy sauce, he only informs me
of his private opinion concerning it.   It admits
of no reasoning, pro or con. There it must rest,
and he must have the like patience to hear me,
in my turn, declare that gravy sauce is far before currant ; and this without making any re-
ply, if he has a grain of sense. It is quite otherwise when either he or I assert that Westminster hall is longer than Westminster bridge, or
that oak is specifically heavier than copper ; for
in each of those cases there is a standard to apply, to wit, a foot rule in one case, and a pair
of scales in the other, which entirely exclude
opinion from having any share in the debate.
With regard to one thing's being comparatively
better than another, there is likewise a standard of another kind, which leaves the preference to be decided by the judgment ; and that
is the relation which such things bear to the use
for which they are both supposed to be intended.   As for instance, if it should become the
subject of enquiry which of two swords is the
best, the intention of fighting being supposed,
the preference will be reasonably given to that,
which, by its superior strength, lightness, sharp-
ness, and perhaps length, is the fittest for fight.
If, for the same purpose, the comparison happens between a sword and a pair of scissars, the

pre-

preference will, no doubt, fall to the fword for very obvious reafons. But vary the circumftances of the intended combat, and explain that it is not to be fought in a field, but in a poft chaife or a centry box, and you will be obliged to rejudge the caufe by a new ftandard, which will infallibly declare a pair of fciffars to be a more fatal, and confequently a better, weapon than any Toledo in the world. It is poffible, by thus fuppofing certain circumftances, to bring the moft different and moft remote objects in nature to be compared by a common ftandard; but where this is not provided, reafon muft be pleafed to leave the bench, and refer the matter entirely to tafte, or private inclination. It is that alone which can determine a young Lady in her choice between pink and blue, or perhaps between her Dancing-mafter, and the Sheriff of the County; and from fuch a fentence there lies no appeal. Having thus, as I think, fairly ftated the different pretenfions of judgment and tafte, I will leave it to your Lordfhip to pronounce whether they are fo like one another as to be eafily miftaken.

Lord MODISH.

In the way you have ftated the affair there can be no difficulty, and the maxim, that *there is no difputing of taftes,* is one of thofe that are the moft univerfally received.

Col. FREEMAN.

The maxim is, as you fay, my Lord, in every body's mouth, but there are very few whofe
under-

underſtandings are at all the better for it. I
have, you know, in the courſe of my life, mixed in a great variety of ſcenes, civil and military,
and have made one in all ſorts of companies,
from her Grace's drawing-room to a Graveſend
tilt-boat, but have ever found, at leaſt, three
fourths of the converſations, high and low, to
be employed in each perſon's declaring his own
taſte, and decrying that of his companions: a
method of ſpending time which appeared to me
ſo uninterefting, ſo unentertaining, and ſo un-
profitable, that it has contributed more than
any thing elſe to the ſolitary and bookiſh life
that I have led for ſome years paſt. Not but
that I find, every now and then, ſome of my
calf-ſkin companions, who are guilty of the ſame
egotiſms, impertinently endeavouring to palm
upon me their own opinions and thoſe of their
maſters, inſtead of argument and matter of fact;
but then I can more eaſily get rid of their company. I was laſt Sunday drinking tea at Lady
Faddleton's, where unfortunately Miſs Molly
Bright happened to be mentioned as a beauty,
and produced a diſpute of an hour and a half,
that made me ſorry the holineſs of the day did
not ſuffer me to propoſe whiſt; for I think a total ſilence not ſo bad as ſo perverſe an abuſe of
ſpeech.

LADY HARRIOT.

And pray, Colonel, don't you think Miſs
Molly Bright handſome?

COL.

Col. FREEMAN.

Suppose, Madam, I should say yes ; what would your Ladyship infer from my answer? Nothing more, I presume, than that she was handsome in my eyes. Were you desirous of knowing what she appeared in my Lord's, I fancy you would be under a necessity of putting the same question to him, just as if it had never been put to me.

Lady HARRIOT.

Then you think it is all fancy, and that there is nothing real in beauty.

Col. FREEMAN.

I have, Madam, too much reason to believe that there is something real in its effects, if you will accept of that as an answer.

Lady HARRIOT.

I am not philosopher enough to know whether it be an answer or not. But sure, Colonel, you must own there are some women whom all the world allows to be handsome.

Col. FREEMAN.

Your Ladyship seems to be more a philosopher than you are willing to acknowledge. You are endeavouring, I find, to withdraw female beauty from amongst the number of those things which are merely the objects of taste, by

an

an appeal to a matter of fact, the general sentiments of mankind. But, suppofing the fact to be conclufive, I do not underftand how it can be fo afcertained as to become a fafe foundation for any fuperftructure of reafoning.

Lady MODISH.

Perhaps, Colonel, you do not allow there is fuch a thing neither as uglinefs. Could you prove that point, there are fome Ladies whom the whole town would think vaftly beholden to you.

Col. FREEMAN.

The cafe of deformity is fomewhat different, Madam, from that of beauty. Deformity may be fubject to enquiry, and reducible to certain principles, altho' beauty fhould not. A face which has one eye larger than the other, which has the mouth awry, or one cheek fat and the other lean, is certainly deformed, and in this all men will agree. But it does not follow that the reverfe of thefe will produce beauty. As to the agreement which Lady Harriot has obferved with regard to the beauty of certain females, I believe it will not be difficult to account for it without allowing it to be real. As for inftance, let us fuppofe that two or three of thofe worthies, who are by fate appointed to fet fafhions in our great city, fhould from amongft five thoufand young women, equally free of deformity, pick out Mifs Thingum, at random, and toaft her upon all occa-

occaſions for a burning beauty. What will be the conſequence? Thoſe who are an inch below them in faſhionability, if you will allow me the word, will catch the ſound, and convey it like the watch-word of a camp from the Generaliſ-ſimo to the centinel. The machine being once ſet in motion, there is nothing to obſtruct its pro-greſs. The men of ſenſe never tire other people with declaring their own taſtes, and are equally unwilling to loſe their time in diſputing the taſtes of others. Amongſt the fools there is here and there one to be found, who will en=gage in the wiſe controverſy, and will ſay, *In-deed I don't ſee any thing ſo ſuperlatively hand-ſome in Miſs Thingum, that there ſhould be all this rout made about her*; but the greateſt part of them are ſuch poltroons as to be afraid of oppoſing the prevailing cry for fear of ſhewing their ignorance, always ſuppoſing beauty to be a ſcience which it is incumbent upon every gen-tleman to underſtand. This I am ſure of, that there is nothing more common, both for fools and men of ſenſe, than when their toaſt is demanded, to give a faſhionable beauty whom they never ſaw. As to the Ladies, tho'.none of them can be ſuppoſed much ſmitten with Miſs Thingum, yet they are all unanimous in allowing her to be handſome, and this from a very obvious motive. They all know that any heſitation from them would be aſcribed to envy, which, as it would both leſſen them-

ſelves,

felves, and add to the triumph of their rival, they are at a great deal of pains to hide; and all the while that they look upon her fway as ufurpation, they, for their own fakes, affert her divine right. Mankind upon many fuch occafions become their own dupes, and fall proftrate before the idols which themfelves have fet up; but hiftory, Lady Harriot, and the inveftigation of facts will always enable us to fet the true ftamp upon fuch fublime pretenfions. Whatever is natural is of divine origin, and the firft fource of it will be for ever hid from our vain curiofity; but all fham claims to divinity are eafily expofed, whenever the proper means are employed. Would you, for inftance, be certified whether any particular race of Kings are by divine appointment, you need only trace their fteps, and it is ten to one but you find the firft of them at the head of a gang of rebels, murderers, and banditti. The fame method of enquiry will fet us right, as to the unbounded empire which town-toafts pretend to exercife over our hearts. A very little tracing will convince us, that altho' they are women by the eternal appointment of the Almighty, they owe their being, as univerfal beauties, to a very few men, and thofe perhaps neither the wifeft nor the fobereft of their fpecies. At leaft we may in this manner account for the apparent univerfality of fentiment concerning them, to a degree that will render

it

it too doubtful for any conclufion to be drawn from it.

Lord MODISH.

My dear Colonel, your hiftory of Mifs Thingum, as you call her, is very plaufible; but you have not given us the proof of any of thofe facts by which you pretend to trace the progrefs of her glory. You feem here, I think, to give more indulgence to your own guefles than you are commonly willing to allow to thofe of other people.

Col. FREEMAN.

Your objection, my Lord, is very juft; and as I knew not how to ftrip thofe general facts of the appearance of guefles, I was not very pofitive in my inferences from them. My notion, however, of that matter is formed from real obfervations, ftrong enough from their number to convince myfelf; tho' fingly too inconfiderable, to be of weight in a queftion of fo general a nature, or to be urged as proof to your Lordfhip: unlefs your experience happen to coincide with mine; which I am apt to believe is in fome meafure the cafe, by your allowing my account to be plaufible. But I have an argument much more clearly founded againft the agreement of mankind, with regard to the beauty of any particular female; which is, that fuch an univerfality of fentiments would ftand in contradiction to all the

B   hitherto

hitherto known principles of nature: for it would have been given in vain, if not for very deftructive purpofes. For what could be fuppofed more ridiculous, and even fatal, than for all the inhabitants of London and Weftminfter to be real, inftead of pretended, admirers of one woman ? Happily for the world, their practice, which is much more to be depended on than their words, fhews us that this is far from being the cafe; and that each of them has his fair, for whom he fighs in private, and whofe name he thinks too facred to be mingled with the ribaldry and midnight debauch of a tavern.

Lady HARRIOT.

That may be very true, Colonel; but may not a man think a woman beautiful without being in love with her? and on the contrary, may he not be in love with one whom he does not think beautiful? There is a thing they call the agreeable, which has often more powerful effects than mere beauty.

Lord MODISH.

Harriot is certainly in the right there, George; I believe there is no body but has, fome time or other, felt that diftinction.

Col. FREEMAN.

My Lord, I have often heard the diftinction; but I am apt to fufpect that it confifts
                                    only

only in the oppofition of real fentiment to miftaken knowledge; or rather, of a word with a
meaning to one that has little or none.

Lord MODISH.

I fhould be glad to have that explained.

Col. FREEMAN.

Indeed, my Lord, the diftinction betwixt
beautiful and agreeable, when applied to faces, is barely verbal, and will vanifh, together with all the difficulties attending this
fubject, immediately upon a precife definition
of thofe words. We have only to afk ourfelves, what is *beauty*? The philofophical
anfwer, is, *That form which pleafes.* Let us
next afk, what is meant by an agreeable form;
the anfwer is certainly, *That which pleafes.* So
that to determine which of the two, the beautiful or the agreeable woman, when put in
oppofition, is the genuine beauty, we need
only examine the actual effects of both; and
if it appears that love and defire are attendant
upon agreeable women no lefs than upon
beauties, as both your Lordfhip and Lady
Harriot feem to allow, it will follow that the
agreeable woman is really beautiful in the eyes
of that man to whom fhe is agreeable, any
reafoning or fafhion to the contrary notwithftanding.

Lord

Lord MODISH.

Suppofing your notion of the agreeable to be juft, I fhould be glad to know what is then meant by beauty in oppofition to what pleafes only. You know it is a word in every body's mouth, and you cannot imagine they mean nothing at all by it. If I were inclined to doubt them, my own fentiments would convince me of their fincerity. Is there no fuch thing as regular features, which may fatisfy the judgment, without touching the heart?

Col. FREEMAN.

I have many reafons, my Lord, to believe there is not, but, without having recourfe to any, the difcourfe of thofe who value themfelves the moft upon their connoiffeurfhip in beauty, is fufficient to convince us that they talk with as little reflection as feeling upon the fubject. Afk one of them what he means by *regular* features; he will firft be furprized at your ignorance; and if you perfift in your enquiry, will tell you, *features that are in due proportion*; afk what he means by due proportion, and he will perhaps tell you, after much ftammering, *that Lady fomebody's features are in due proportion*; afk why he thinks her features in due proportion, he will tell you, *becaufe they are regular*; and if you carry on your queftions to all eternity, the anfwers will ftill trot

in

in the same circle they set out in; and tho'
very far from making us more knowing than
we were, are perhaps the best answers that the
the subject affords. The folly lies in answer-
ing at all to such questions.——You seem in
deep contemplation, my Lord.

Lord MODISH.

Faith, George, I was first rummaging my
brain to see whether I could not find there
some rules by which features might be adjust-
ed; but to no purpose. From that I have gone
upon a more humble search, to try if I could
discover what it was that had all along induced
me to speak of such things. For I assure you
I meant something; tho', to deal sincerely, I
am not able, at this time, to tell what. Are
you conjuror enough to guess what I meant?

Col. FREEMAN.

If my knowledge and penetration were
equal to your Lordship's candor I should not
despair, however difficult the task, of giving
you complete satisfaction. But as it is only a
guess you demand, you shall have it, hit or
miss; and the more readily as this is not the first
time I have endeavoured to account to myself,
for so whimsical a phenomenon in human nature.
A very little sedate reflection must convince a
man of sense that there is no standard of female
beauty, to which all the various degrees of it may
be referred; and yet it is no less plain that those

who

who every day so earnestly dispute about those
various degrees, must have something which
they persuade themselves is a standard. The
question is only, how they came by such a
persuasion? My conjecture is, that it is acquired by early education, and so early, that
no man is able to remember its first establish-
ment in his mind. I suppose a child of two
years old is told that *Mis what do you call it*,
whom he sees perhaps every day, is vastly
handsome. This being the first time of his
learning the word handsome or beautiful, and
connecting an idea to it, he will never after be
able to separate the word from its original
impression; but will, from that accidental con-
junction, form to himself a general system of
beauty, and will keep it up, by a successive application of it to other women, many years after she who give birth to his system is forgot-
ten. And thus by a perverse adherence to
theory, in a matter entirely practical, he will
persist to his dying day in extolling a certain
sort of faces for which he has not the least desire or affection. In this manner five hundred
men may have five hundred standards of beauty; which tho' all taken from women without
any deformity or just exception, may be all
exceedingly different from one another. What
wonder is it then that one man's verdict upon
a woman's beauty should be so little satisfactory
to his companion, who measures her by another

other scale. This cannot be called *disputing tastes*; becaufe tafte or fentiment is here entirely excluded; but it is equally ufelefs and irrational.

Such, however, feem to be the grounds upon which the common run of mankind venture to give their judgment in thofe matters. With regard to the more inftructed and polite, there is another circumftance, which, having more the appearance of a common ftandard, has abundantly affifted in running them into difputes concerning beauty; and that is the agreement of painters and fculptors upon that head; which they fuppofe could not happen, if every artift was left to his own particular feeling of beauty, without any principles to guide him. But it is very eafy to account for this agreement, without finding ourfelves much nearer an univerfal ftandard than we were at firft. No fooner were the arts of painting and fculpture brought to fome degree of excellence, but the artifts, in reprefenting a Venus, an Helen, or any other perfonage, from whom beauty was expected, muft have found all their endeavours to pleafe rendered ineffectual by the variety of fentiments which different men, by the various ftructure of their nerves and organs, have of beauty: fo that the painter's miftrefs however beautiful fhe might appear to him, and however juftly he might portray her, would have little chance of charming the fpectators,

who

who would each think his own Dulcinea infinitely superior to the Venus. Neither would he mend the matter by substituting a beauty of his judgment, according to the method just described, whilst every man had a standard of his own, equally partial, by which he condemned it. Here necessity, the mother of invention, would come to his assistance, and set him upon a method that, although it might charm few, would disgust no body; that is, to form a face that should affect a medium in all its features and proportions, carefully avoiding every thing extraordinary, however himself might be struck with it. He must have found that tho' one man, either by a peculiarity of real taste, or of acquired prepossession, was fond of a high nose; another thought it detestable. That to one a fat cheek was charming, to another a lean one, and that each despised the other's choice as deformed and ridiculous. The painter's business was therefore to steer as clear as possible of these opposite rocks, and to give his goddess neither a high nor a low, but a streight nose, with cheeks that were neither fat nor lean, preserving the same mediocrity in all the proportions of her face. Upon such a principle as this we may suppose it was that Polycletus formed his Venus, which Pliny says was called the canon or standard; and that he actually

did

did fo, ftill farther appears by all the antique ftatues now remaining; which, by their great fimilarity, plainly appear to be all copies, more or lefs exact, of one original, framed upon this cautious principle. But it is one thing not to be deformed, and another to be beautiful; one thing to avoid cenfure, and another thing to pleafe. Neither have I met with ought in the opinions of the eminent painters and fculptors, with whom I am ufed to converfe, that any way inclines me to alter mine with regard to this matter. Thofe of them who have fpent fome of their beft years in the ftudy of the antique ftatues, and the modern imitations of them all over Italy, have told me that upon their firft acquaintance they were not fo much ftruck with the beauty of their faces; but that the more they faw them, the more their admiration of them encreafed. But this after-admiration is far from being a proof of their having any thing remarkably beautiful in themfelves; and is nothing more than the common effect of habit, which fhews itfelf not only in things of an indifferent nature, fuch as cookery, drefs, and furniture, but often alfo in things that are at firft extremely naufeous and difagreeable, fuch as tobacco, coffee, and other drugs, which by ufe become fo bewitching, that their votaries rather chufe to part with their health than refign them. Here then, in the antique, we find a fort of common meafure,

but

but which falls mightily in its value when we consider that it is only of a negative kind, from which no excellence, no striking grace can be expected: and likewise that, imperfect as it is, it is known only to a few, perhaps not one in a hundred of those who talk about regular features; and of those few there is still a much smaller number, chiefly painters and sculptors, on whom the habit of looking at those antiques has been so constant as to make any real impression. In such it may be called their taste; but, as I hinted some time ago, we must be careful not to say that such people have a good or a bad taste; since whatever is truly taste, whether it belonged originally to the nerves, or was produced in them by habit, admits of no comparison, in point of excellence. All we can say with propriety is, that such a man has the tobacco taste, or the sugar-candie taste, or the antique taste; that is, he likes tobacco, sugar-candie, or the antique. This has in it nothing comparative, and is only an assertion concerning a matter of fact of the simplest kind.

But, my Lord, I find my eagerness in endeavouring to satisfy your Lordship's demand, has led me into a Professorial kind of discourse, that will be little agreeable, I am afraid, to the Ladies. It is the common effect of such subjects; so let us call a new cause. Pray, Lady Modish, has your Ladyship seen the two new dancers that Rich has brought over?

LADY

Lady MODISH.

Whether I have, or have not, I fha'n't tell you. And truly, Colonel, you ought to make us fome apology for breaking off a ferious converfation upon our account; as if we were incapable of being entertained by any thing but trifles. It is true we are feldom tried with any thing elfe, but that is not fo much our fault as that of you men; who think, no doubt, to preferve your authority the better by keeping us in ignorance.

Lady HARRIOT.

Indeed, Colonel, the conclufion of your fpeech does not deferve, either from my fifter or me, any acknowledgments that are favourable; and yet, fuch is my goodnefs, I cannot help owning that I have been much better entertained with your explanation of tafte, than ever I was with any of thofe difputes which it daily occafions. Moft men, indeed, who enter upon nice fubjects before Ladies, feem rather, by their latin and cramp words, to aim at aftonifhing, than either entertaining or inftructing us. But I muft do you the juftice to fay that this is never your practice; for you always exprefs yourfelf in fo plain a way that I fancy I comprehend your whole meaning, tho' it is probable I am fometimes miftaken.

Col.

Col. FREEMAN.

I acknowledge, Ladies, both the juſtice and gentleneſs of your rebuke, and am perfectly ſenſible that, if I am not underſtood in a ſubject like this, which is not peculiar to any art or profeſſion, the defect is in me, and not in either of your Ladyſhips. And as for the cramp words Lady Harriot mentions, they are ſeldom any thing but ſkreens which vanity has hitherto employed in order to hide ignorance. Of late, philoſophy has put on a more familiar air, and is not aſhamed to have it known that ſhe is nothing but common ſenſe and experience methodiſed ; and it ſeems now agreed that the truly learned language is that which is beſt underſtood.

Lord MODISH.

I muſt own, Colonel, that the notion of an univerſal ſtandard for the beauty of natural objects, would be very contradictory to that almoſt ſelf-evident truth, that *whatever is is right*; ſince in the great variety of forms which God has contrived, the benign end of pleaſing would have been fruſtrated, if he had not ordained a like variety to exiſt in the apprehenſions and feelings of different men as well as of different animals concerning thoſe things.

Col. FREEMAN.

It is moſt certainly ſo, my Lord ; and it is ſurprizing that ſo many ingenious men ſhould have

have loft their time in a search, the vanity of which is so obvious. Hogarth owns that his line of beauty and grace is not to be seen in a toad; which if true, ought to have convinced him, either that there was no such line, or universal receipt for beauty; or else that he had not yet hit upon it: since it hardly admits of a doubt, that a blooming she toad is the most beautiful fight in the creation, to all the crawling young gentlemen of her acquaintance; and that her crawl, or as they may possibly call it, her *pas grave*, is far before the minuet step, with all its wavings. An analysis or dissection can never be begun of any subject till the subject itself is ascertained, and consequently no analysis can be made of abstract beauty, nor of any abstraction whatsoever. Till a real something is discovered, which we are sure by experience is universally the source of pleasure, any attempt to discover the universal principle of pleasure by analysis must be fruitless; and the philosopher who engages in such a business, after finding that he has been gravely measuring a dream with a pair of compasses, will probably return at last to the *je ne scay quoy*, upon which he had at first disdainfully turned his back. Does your Lordship know Sir Roger North?

Lord MODISH.

Yes, a little; he seems to be a comical hearty old fellow.

Col.

Col. FREEMAN.

He is so, my Lord; but he is something more; for he is a man of a good deal of learning and reflection; though, by a strange turn of temper, he seems to be at pains to conceal it, and when his good sense makes its appearance, it is commonly under the disguise of waggery. I happened to be walking in the Mall with Sir Harry Beaumont, about a week after Crito was published, when Sir Roger came up to us, and, after congratulating his brother Baronet upon the success of his performance, and the figure it was like to give him in the eyes of the Misses, as an arbiter of beauty, Sir Harry, says he, I observe that in your distribution of grace you give twenty degrees to Mrs. A***, and thirty to Mrs. B***. Now I do not find fault with your tables, but I should be glad to know by what scale, weight, or measure you compute their several shares with so much precision. You certainly, answered Sir Harry, did not read my paper with much attention, or else you would have seen that *I did not pretend to have made my calculations exactly*; but rather *to point out what might be done by more exact judges of beauty*. Ay, but, Sir Harry, says the old Knight, let who will calculate those tables of beauty, it will have but a very unscholarlike appearance, if, when the exactness of their calculations happens to be called in question, they

should

ſhould have nothing better to appeal to, than the infallibility of their own judgments. I am afraid that method would hardly paſs muſter at the Royal Society. Now, you muſt know, when I was a boy I was a great dab at figures, and though I ſeldom foul my fingers with pen and ink, I have not yet forgot the rules, and have been thinking that the rule of three or rule of proportion, might be applied ſo as to become a golden rule in comparing beauties as much as any thing elſe. It is performed, you know, by multiplying the firſt by the ſecond, and dividing by the third; and being curious this morning to know with exactneſs how much Mrs. D * * * excelled in beauty Mrs. C * * *, I thus ſtated the queſtion, *as a cat is to a wheel-barrow ſo is Mrs. C * * * to Mrs. D * * *;* but though I tried till my brain was ready to crack, I never could contrive how to multiply a cat by a wheel-barrow; ſo I could go no farther in my calculations. Now if you, or any other virtuoſo, could fall upon the method of multiplying and dividing ſuch matters; I am perſuaded you would find out a certain method of gauging every woman's beauty, and *prevent it from being any longer left,* as you juſtly complain, *to the particular whim of ignorant people.* Sir Harry was a little ſtunn'd with this whimſical attack, but he did not loſe his good humour, and only ſaid, I ſee you are ſtill the old man, Sir Roger; what ſhould be grave you con-

conftantly turn to farce; and then left us to run
after Mifs Hoyden, who was croffing towards
the palace. When he was gone, fays Sir Roger
to me, Our friend Sir Harry may defpife the
old proverb as much as he will, but fuch
comparifons will always be *odious*, and it is no
wonder, for they will always be abfurd.

Lord MODISH.

I believe, indeed, we muft leave the beauties
of nature, where every thing is perfeᏟ in itfelf,
to every one's particular tafte, without attempt-
ing to difpute or compare them. But if I give
you up that, I hope you will allow us that there
may be a good or a bad tafte where the contrivance of man has had a part. What fay you,
for inftance, to a good tafte in architeᏟure?

Col. FREEMAN.

The fame, my Lord, that I fhould fay to a
good tafte in drefs or cookery, that, abftraᏟed
from health and conveniency, which are the
objeᏟs of reafon, it is one of thofe taftes which
cuftom, a fecond nature, has beftowed upon
us; and is fo much mere tafte that it can never,
with any propriety, become a matter of difpute
or comparifon. To infift upon one form of
drefs, or one form of building, being in itfelf
more beautiful than another, muft appear to a
philofopher entering upon as fenflefs a controverfy, as the pretending that one difh was in itfelf

felf more palatable than another, and that he
who preferred the one had a better tafte than
he who preferred the other.

Lord MODISH.

But fure, Colonel, there are rules for the
beauties of architecture, and not the fmalleft
ornament of a bafe or cornifh without its fettled
proportion.

·Col. FREEMAN.

Were that ftrictly the cafe, my Lord, we
fhould call it knowledge or judgment in architecture, not tafte ; for, as far as thefe rules go,
no tafte is required, either good or bad. An
Artift may, by a Palladian receipt alone, without any tafte, form a very elegant Corinthian
pillar; as a cook, without any palate, and by
the help of the *houfewife's vade mecum* only,
makes an unexceptionable difh of *beef a la
daube*. Thefe rules are plainly no more than
the analyfis of certain things which cuftom has
rendered agreeable ; but do not point out to us
any natural ftandard of beauty or flavour, by
which fuch things, whether pillars or difhes,
could have been originally contrived to anfwer
the purpofe of pleafing. I fhould be exceedingly glad to hear a reafon why a Corinthian capital clapt upon its fhaft upfide-down fhould not
become, by cuftom, as pleafing a fpectacle as
in the manner it commonly ftands. I know
this would be look'd upon as a fort of blafphemy

C   by

by fome of our dilettanti; but fo is every opinion, however reafonable, which oppofes what is by cuftom eftablifhed in any country. Perhaps there are countries in the world where my capital is fo much in tafte, that their virtuofi would be furprized to hear that there was any nation fo abfurd as to put the volutes uppermoft. At leaft there is no imagination of that fort fo odd that fome fimilar experience is not fufficient to juftify and render probable.

Lord MODISH.

How then came the prefent fafhion (fince you will have it to be no better) of architecture to be fo univerfally embraced?

Col. FREEMAN.

It's univerfality, my Lord, does not extend beyond Chriftendom; and, if it fhould become the tafte of the whole univerfe, the fame means, which have procured it a reception among us, will account for its further progrefs, without our giving ourfelves the trouble of fearching for any ftandard in nature for its recommendation. It is the nature of all fafhions (I except only thofe of a religious kind) to take their rife from the fovereign will and pleafure of the rich and powerful. Men in fuch circumftances are known from thence to acquire a prefumption, which naturally induces them to take the lead in every thing; while thofe very

cir-

circumſtances which engage them to indulge
their caprices, enable them at the ſame time
to render thoſe caprices reſpeᦄtable. As for
inſtance, let a man of ordinary rank or figure
appear in publick in a coat whoſe cuffs are triangular, when the mode is ſquare; and there
is no doubt he will meet with many to deſpiſe,
but none to imitate him. Let the ſame be
tried by a man bleſt with title, riches, youth,
and all the trappings of proſperity; let the ſleeve
be of velvet, curiouſly embroidered, and part
of a ſuit of cloaths in all other reſpeᦄts faſhionable and rich, the triangle will then be found to
meet with a quite different reception, and tho'
feeble in itſelf, will be ſo powerfully ſeconded
by, being incorporated with, the title, the em-
broidery, the coach, and the footman, as to
become part of the auguſt idea of his grace;
and ſo far from being able to render him ridiculous, will receive a ſhare of reſpeᦄt by being
part of him; and from being tolerable, will
ſoon become an objeᦄt of imitation, eſpecially
to the perſons who are the moſt intimate with
him and his cloaths. The more thoſe imitations encreaſe, the more the ſenſation of their
beauty is confirmed; till, in a ſhort time, all
other cuffs but the triangular are deteſtable. City
taylors bribe his Lordſhip's valet de chambre
to let them take it's ſhape and proportions;
and here is, at laſt, a preciſe rule eſtabliſh-
ed.

Lord

Lord MODISH.

My dear George, this is a lamentable fink-
ing from architecture to cuffs.

Col. FREEMAN.

I do that, my Lord, in imitation of fome
great men of our acquaintance, who let themfelves down very low in order to rife with the
more fecurity. The progrefs of fafhion in drefs,
and the feelings which are the confequence of
that progrefs, being the moft familiar, and having at the fame time the quickeft revolutions,
are of all others the fitteft to explain the nature
of fafhion in general. The fafhions in building,
tho' more durable than thofe in drefs, are not
for that the lefs fafhions, and are equally fubject to change. But as ftones and bricks are
more lafting than filk and velvet, and as people
do not make up churches and palaces fo often
as they do coats and capuchines, we muft have
recourfe to hiftory for the knowledge of thofe
changes, which we can learn but very imper-
fectly from our own proper experience. In hiftory we fhall find that every nation received
it's mode of architecture from that nation which,
in all other refpects, was the higheft in credit,
riches, and general eftimation. The admiration that attends whatever is great in its dimen-
fions, coftly in its materials, and precife in its
execution, is, as far as our experience goes,
univerfal; and naturally inclines the mind in
favour of any form which accident has com-
bined

bined with thofe admirable qualities. The Egyptians were the firft people we know of who were fo rich, and at their eafe, as to build with grandeur, coft, and neatnefs ; and from thence infpired the Greeks with a love for thofe ornaments which their caprice had added to the ufeful part of architecture. The Greeks, in their turn, becoming for many ages a free, a rich, and a happy people, had an opportunity of practifing thofe arts in many fumptuous buildings; where, befide the invention of arches, and other folid improvements in the art of building, they made many changes, as their fancy led them, upon the Egyptian ornaments. In this ftate was architecture when it was tranf-planted to Rome, by a people who, by perpetual wars, had in a fhort time attained from the meaneft origin, to the greateft height of power. Deftitute of money, and profoundly ignorant of all the arts of peace, they had never raifed any buildings of which they could boaft ; and no fooner had they an opportunity of confidering the Grecian temples and other public works, great in themfelves, and fet off with all that coftly materials and the genius of their excellent painters and fculptors could add to the fkill of the mafon, but ftruck with the complex object, they decreed the Greeks to be the only architects in the world, and fubmitted willingly to receive laws in the arts from thofe whom their Arms had fubdued. Perhaps the philofo-

C 3   phy,

phy, poetry, and mufic of Greece, for which they began at the fame time to take a relifh, ferved not a little to raife the reputation of the Greeks, and might ftrengthen their authority in architecture; tho' not neceffarily connected with them. An admiration, to a degree of bigotry feized the Roman artifts and connoifeurs, and put an effectual ftop to any farther change or improvement in architecture. Their fole ftudy was to imitate the Grecian buildings, and the being like or unlike to them became foon the meafure of right and wrong. Rules fo compiled were committed to writing, and continue to this day, together with fome of the antient buildings upon which they were formed, to be the ftandard of tafte all over chriftendom. Time may poffibly produce on it infenfible changes, but there is almoft nothing which can be imagined to give it a total overthrow, unlefs Europe fhould become a conqueft of the Chinefe.

Lord MODISH.

If the five orders of architecture with all their paraphernalia are to reign in fplendor, till we are conquered by the Chinefe, they need be under little apprehenfion. But, my dear Colonel, allowing this chimerical conqueft of yours to take place, why muft our architecture be deftroyed along with our freedom? Why may we not as well fuppofe that our conquerors fhould receive the fafhion in

those

thofe matters from us, as you fay the conquering Romans did from the Greeks?

Col. FREEMAN.

Becaufe, my Lord, the circumftances of the conquerors and the conquered would be very different. In China the arts of peace have been long cultivated, and they have been long charmed with buildings, which though of a tafte very bad, according to our notions, are yet more extenfive and more fumptuoufly adorned than ours. It would be no wonder, then, if they refufed to change that form of building which long ufage had rendered graceful, for one which had all the awkwardnefs of novelty, without any other advantage to dazle and prepoffefs them in its favour. To them the fimplicity of the antique would appear mean and ruftic; and Covent-Garden church, the pride of Englifh architecture, would be judged fitter for a barn than a temple. Neither do I mention this to your Lordfhip upon bare conjecture, but from the fimilar experience of what formerly happened in Europe when it was overrun by the Goths. I fee you fmile at the mention of my friends the Goths; but allow me to tell your Lordfhip the Goths were not fo Gothic as they are generally imagined. The arts, indeed, of poetry and painting feem to have been unknown or neglected among them; but in that they could be little worfe than the peo-

ple

ple they overcame, and in fome other refpects they were much their fuperiors. Civil difcord, and all the evils that attend anarchy when joined to a moft contemptible fuperftition, had produced in the Roman empire a poverty of every kind, and an almoft total obliteration of thofe arts and fciences for which the fame nations had been, but a few centuries before, fo juftly celebrated. Among the Gothic nations the art of war was well underftood, as appears by their conftant fuperiority, whenever they appeared in the field ; and all the ftates of Europe, who at this day enjoy any of the bleffings of good government, are ready to own that from this Gothic fource thofe bleffings were derived. But they were not like the Romans, a gang of meer plunderers, fprung from thofe who had been, but a little while before their conqueft of Greece, naked thieves and runaway flaves; but a colony from an empire, no lefs than that of the Parthians, which had long fubfifted in fplendor and magnificence; and which, in eftablifhing itfelf upon the ruins of the empire of Perfia, had fucceeded to the greateft part of its riches, luxury, and elegance. It is in Parthia or Perfia that we muft look for the origin of thofe fhoals of warlike men, and for the origin of that tafte of architecture of which the ftately examples ftill remain, like fo many trophies to mark the progrefs of their victories. And if we turn our eyes to the feats of the prefent Sophi

of

of Perſia, we ſhall there ſee the pointed arch, and all the other parts of what we call Gothic architecture, ſtill in high faſhion, and ſtudded over, as Milton ſays, *with barbaric pearl and gold*.

Lord MODISH.

I do remember, now you put me in mind of it, to have ſeen at Sir John Locke's, a collection of drawings repreſenting bridges, palaces, and moſques, done, as he told me, from the buildings themſelves, while he was reſident at Iſpahan ; and which very well correſpond with what you ſay concerning the likeneſs between the Perſian and Gothic taſte of architecture. But I ſhould not think that likeneſs, however ſtrong, a ſufficient proof, that thoſe, who have been always called Northern nations, were really the ſons of the Eaſt.

Col. FREEMAN.

There are, my Lord, a great many other proofs of the Parthic or Perſian extraction of the Goths to be gathered from the ſimilitude of language and manners, and even from the hiſtory of their migration. Some of theſe proofs, as they accidentally occurred to me in my reading, I have been at the pains to commit to paper, and ſhall communicate them to your Lordſhip upon your return to London, if your curioſity leads you to the enquiry. But whether they came from Perſia or Peru, it is plain from the ſight of the firſt public buildings

5   erect-

erected by them, upon their entrance into the
Roman provinces, that they came from some
great and established empire, where the art of
building with grandeur and magnificence had
been, by the practice of many ages, brought to
an uncommon degree of perfection. Structures
such as Westminster Abbey, with which Ger-
many, France, and Spain abound, so extensive,
yet so neat, so strong, and yet so richly, nay
sometimes finically ornamented, can never be
supposed the contrivance of hungry soldiers, during their march through the enemies country;
nor of obscure savages, just escaped from under
the snows of Sweden and Norway. Such arts
are not so suddenly brought to perfection as to
be the offspring of one man's brain; and if they
were, yet the concurrence of all the different
branches of those invaders, whether Vandals,
Huns, Saxons, Normans, or Franks, in the
same forms and decorations, plainly shew that
there were certain antient and established rules
for those things, which they all equally knew
and respected. To men, thus prepossessed with
ideas both grand and precise, the buildings they
met with in the Roman provinces must have
appeared mean and flat; and if they destroyed
any of them without hesitation, whenever they
stood in their way, it must not be attributed to
their barbarous insensibility of what was elegant;
but to their overweening fondness for their own
taste, and unreasonable desire of imposing it upon

on others: a malady, which the moſt poliſhed people when unreſtrained by reaſoning and re-flection, are equally ſubject to, with the moſt ſavage.

Lord MODISH.

That the Goths did make their taſte of archi-tecture the reigning taſte over Europe for ſeveral ages, I very well know. But, my dear George, your reaſon for its taking place of the Grecian, is not at all ſatisfactory ; for if it bore it down at firſt by its loftineſs and richneſs, it might, with much more eaſe, have maintained its ſuperiority, after being familiariſed by time to the conquered, as well as to their invaders. I ſhould conclude, therefore, from the reſtoration of the Greek architecture, that it had ſomething in its forms peculiarly adapted to pleaſe the ſight, which made it at length ſurmount all the obſtacles which force and cuſtom had thrown in its way.

Col. FREEMAN.

Your doubts, my Lord, are exceedingly juſt, and I do not believe that any degree of know-ledge in lines and numbers would ever be able to ſolve them. But there are many ſeeming myſteries, and which continue ſuch againſt all the powers of abſtract reaſoning, which hiſtory, by leading us ſtep by ſtep, renders plain and ſimple. For many ages had biſhops and barons, monks and knights errant, kept the people of Europe in ſlavery and diſſention. ſloth, igno-

rance

rance and mifery. All the arts which tended to
render life more humane and agreeable, were
utterly difcountenanced and forbid; and thofe
alone kept up and practifed, which were of ufe
in fupporting the pride and power of thofe tyrants. Canon law to defend the wordly pretenfions of church-men, and metaphyfics to promote and defend their fpiritual abfurdities, for
the fame gainful purpofe, were what paffed currently by the name of learning. When thefe
failed, in determining the truth or falfhood of
a propofition, recourfe was had, legally and coolly, to fingle combat; a kind of logic, abfurd
enough in all confcience, and yet perhaps not
the moft abfurd kind then in ufe. Painting and
fculpture were not yet found neceffary to be called in aid of thefe holy cheats; fo no man, as
may well be fuppofed, prefumed to carve or
draw the refemblance of any thing upon earth.
Military architecture fhewed itfelf only in the
caftles of private gentlemen, with moats and
draw-bridges; and the civil was only to be looked for in cathedrals and cloifters. The reft were
all hovels and beggary. At laft, about the four-
teenth century, the cloud of ignorance began to
difperfe. The arrogance and avarice of the
church of Rome had ftretched the cord till it
cracked, and brought on, in feveral parts of
Europe, an enquiry into the fpiritual rights of
mankind, which that corporation had fo grofsly
invaded; and thefe having been fo interwoven
                                        with

with their temporal rights, the enquiry always became the more extensive, the farther it proceeded; so that books, and all the other means of knowledge, became every day more and more in requeſt. About this time the Greeks, flying from the Turks, after the taking of Conſtantinople, brought over their books and language into Italy: which, partly by the countenance and patronage of the family of Medicis, in a little time became a faſhionable part of learning, till then utterly unknown in the Weſt. A like unfortunate cauſe with that which brought over the learned Grecians, had before that time tranſported to Florence ſome Greek painters, bad indeed, but ſufficiently ſkilful to ſow thoſe ſeeds of the art, which, by proper encouragement, firſt at Florence, and afterwards at Rome, Venice, and Bologna, arrived at ſo admirable a degree of perfection. The polite arts, and all the ſeveral branches of true learning, have ſo immediate a connection that they always march together; and it is impoſſible to find any one of them in a tolerable degree, without finding along with it ſome portion of each of the reſt. Thus, at the ſame time that the Greek and Roman claſſics were diligently ſought after, amidſt the duſt and ſcholaſtic nonſenſe of the libraries and convents; the pick-ax was every where employed among the ruins, in ſearch of ſtatues and bas-reliefs, which the ignorance and miſery of the times had ſuffered to lie for ages under ground. At
the

the court of Rome, for the support of whose power some measure of true learning was at last become necessary, these enquiries after the learning and elegance of their heathen ancestors, were carried on with the greatest eagerness; and the rising love of painting, sculpture, and music, was not a little promoted by the use they perceived those arts might be of, in supporting a gainful superstition just ready to fall into contempt. Then it was that the Romans began to cast an eye of admiration upon the noble remains of heathen architecture, with which their city is, to this day, so richly stored. In that imperial city, the Gothic people, tho' they had, oftener than once, committed horrible devastations, had never made any settlement, nor ever raised any fabric. The buildings there had ever been according to the Grecian taste; but that being kept up only by tradition, without any precise rules, it had changed extremely from its original. To effect a total alteration in the fashions of any country, is an exceeding difficult undertaking; but here was only required a reformation, and a reformation that had antiquity and primitive purity for its principles. No sooner, then, was the love of heathen antiquity afloat, but the Bramantes and Michelangelos set themselves with great diligence to measure all the parts of all the antient buildings of Rome, and soon, by the help of Vitruvius, composed a system of architecture, which, as far as it

pre-

pretended to go, brought back the Auguftan age to the mafons and carpenters. Florence, and the reft of the cities of Italy, that were, with refpect to architecture, in almoft the fame ftate with Rome, entered readily into this fcheme of reformation, which, crofling the Alps, with the joint cry of all Italy, at that time the fchool of learning and politenefs, carried every thing before it. And thofe Gothic ftructures, which had fo long lorded it over all other works of ftone and mortar, were now decryed as gigantic and barbarous. Increafe of trade and riches, all over Europe, particularly from the new-difcovered Indies, produced a great number of fumptuous buildings in the new fafhion; fo that the fondnefs for it, which was probably, at firft, no more than an affectation of Italian elegance, grew, in a little time, to be a real tafte or fentiment.

Lord MODISH.

Of buildings did he fpeak, like Solomon, from the Pyramids of Egypt, even to the Banqueting houfe at Whitehall. As I hope to be faved, George, you would make an excellent grand mafter of the free and accepted Mafons, and would prelect upon the wonders of the Letter G, to the aftonifhment of the whole lodge. But, ferioufly, we are all vaftly obliged to you for this fhort hiftory of a long tranfaction, many particulars of which I knew before, but never before heard them connected in fo regular a chain.

chain. What you have faid to prove that the beauties of architecture have no deeper founda-tion than fafhion, that is habit formed upon ca-price, carries with it great appearance of truth. But you philofophy men, when you take up any principle, are very apt to carry it farther than it will go, and to a fingle caufe often afcribe an ef-fect which perhaps proceeds from half a dozen. In many cafes I will allow you that habit has a fhare in forming our fentiments; but is there not likewife an infeparable connection between beau-ty and propriety? And will not that which is fit and fuitable in itfelf, be always more or lefs pleaf-ing to the beholder?—I am afraid I don't exprefs my meaning in the proper terms.

Col. FREEMAN.

Exactly, my Lord, like one of the trade. Such are the very expreffions ufed by the followers of Hutchifon, Shaftfbury, and Plato; who drew, moreover, this very obvious conclufion from them, that, by our different feelings or fenfations of pleafure and diflike, we may fafely pronounce the objects, from whence thofe fenfations arife, to be right or wrong in themfelves, without any farther examination or reflection. Happy fenfe for thofe who are endowed with it, and for which one would willingly renounce all human under-ftanding, which is liable to many errors. What pity is it that fo pleafing an opinion, fo elegant

a fyftem

a fyftem fhould have no foundation in fact! Hold up, for a moment, the mirror of experience to this metaphyfical phantom, and it fhrinks into the nothing from whence it fprung. The approbation of reafon, and the approbation of tafte, which thofe gentlemen have been at fo much pains to unite and confound, will be found in their nature diftinct and feparate, and to be allotted for vifibly different purpofes by the author of our nature. That they often coincide is likewife true; but it is owing to other caufes than their natural and infeparable connection, as will be perceived in examining the cafes where this coincidence does, and where it does not appear. To begin with the moft fimple: The apothecary's prentice brings a dofe of the bark to a man fick of the ague: The reafon and experience of the phyfician, perhaps the patient's own experience, affure him, that fwallowing this drug will reftore him to his health. What fays tafte? That it is the devil of a dofe; that it ought to be put off till to-morrow, and in the mean time calls for t'other bottle of Champaign. Tafte then has no fkill in phyfick. Let us fee next whether tafte, in its more remote and figurative applications, is more clofely allied to fitnefs and utility. Amongft the objects of fight, there are none with which we are fo familiar as thofe which drefs exhibits, nor, as I before obferved to your Lordfhip, fo proper to produce examples for this fubject. And

D   there

there ft will be ever found that our feelings
of pleasure and diflike are conducted entirely
by custom, not only in matters indifferent, but
often in oppofition to what is useful and proper. Pray, Lady Modifh, what would your
Ladyfhip think of our fine gentlemen, if they
were to drefs with their arms naked to the el-
bows?

Lady MODISH.

I fhould certainly think them very fhoek-
ing creatures; at leaft if I may guefs by the
difgufting appearance which butchers and hat-
ters make in the like equipage.

Col. FREEMAN.

Your Ladyfhip, I am perfuaded, fpeaks not
only your own fentiments, but likewife the fentiments of all the ladies in England, upon the
occafion. All would agree unanimoufly, at firft,
in its being an ugly fight; and yet it is impoffi-
ble to find out, in the naked arm of a well-proportioned man, any natural impropriety whence
this fentiment of deformity arifes; nor any that is
not equally, at leaft, attached to the naked arm of
a well-proportioned woman, an object which
is allowed to raife in every one a fentiment
very oppofite. Cuftom alone can account
for this whimfical tafte, which breaks thro'
all rules of reafon and propriety; for a dif-
engagement from fleeves is without doubt
most

most befitting the sex which is the most
active, and destined for robust exercise and
labour; and a close covering, especially in
a cold climate, the most proper for that sex
which suffers most from its inclemency. I
have lived long enough in the world, Ladies,
to see a great many changes in it, particularly with regard to shoe-buckles, which
have been now large, now small, now round,
now square, and all, in their turns, fraught
with beauty and deformity. These changes
are productive of much good to many industrious tradesmen and their families, and,
generally speaking, very indifferent to the
wearers. But I remember, about seven or
eight years ago, the buckles, from the toes,
where they had reigned in splendor some
years before, had insensibly crept up to the
leg; and so great was the desire, in our
smarts, of creating pleasing feelings in the
beholders by an amazing length of foot, that
I have seen many of them limping about
Ranelagh with their buckles above the joint,
and suffering no small torture rather than
they should appear with turpitude in a more
convenient place. Instances of this kind in
architecture are not so easily found. Building is, by its nature, a more serious and
more deliberate affair than dress, and less
subject, one would think, to the influence of
whim; yet it is not altogether destitute of

D 2   ex-

examples, where the eye is pleafed with what is the reverfe of conveniency. For fome of thefe a general caufe, or rather origin, may be affigned. The prefent tafte of architecture was formed, not upon the palaces and dwelling-houfes of the antient Greeks and Romans, of which there were no veftiges at the revival of the arts, but upon their temples and other public buildings, from which the ornamental part has been borrowed and applied to domeftic ufe, in a manner abundantly abfurd, for the moft part; and which, neverthelefs, cuftom has rendered agreeable to the fight. I could name to your Lordfhip feveral houfes, befides my Lord Mayor's, where the defire of charming the paffengers, has induced the architect to darken the principal apartments, by clapping before the windows ftately pillars which fupport nothing, or, which is much the fame, nothing of any ufe. Whatever pains thofe gentlemen may take to dignify the ornamental part of their art by fcientific reafonings about propriety and fitnefs, it will be found at laft to owe all its power of pleafing to cuftom only. Afk one of them by what means it is, that a window pleafes by being longer than it is broad, and a chimney by being broader than it is long; he will tell you, that it is from their natural fitnefs for their feveral purpofes, fuch and fuch being the

nature

nature of light, and such and such being the nature of smoak. But let him be ever so learned in light and smoak, this is but a shallow solution of the difficulty. The plain truth is, that on account of their fitness for their several purposes, they have been from time immemorial so formed; but it is the habit of seeing them constantly so formed, and not their fitness, which produces in us that sense of their beauty. This process will account for all the conjunctions of beauty and propriety, which to most people pass for necessary connections. What is the reason that any heavy body, supported by few and weak pillars, gives us an unpleasing feeling? Because the danger and inconveniency of such a disposition has been long known, and with care avoided; so that the least infringement of the established practice will shock us immediately by its unusualness, without allowing our reason to interfere by a slow discussion of its impropriety. In like manner may we account for all that concerns moral taste and sentiment; which will appear, upon the slightest comparison of the feelings of different nations with regard to behaviour, to be immediately and necessarily dependant upon custom, and but remotely and accidentally connected with right and wrong, or the invariable fitness of things.

D 3

LORD

Lord MODISH.

I begin to be afraid that tafte, at laft, muft content himfelf with ruling over the finer arts. There I think you will hardly try to pull him from his throne.

Col. FREEMAN.

What arts does your Lordfhip comprehend under that title?

Lord MODISH.

Mufic, poetry, and painting; or, as they call them, the fifter arts.

Col. FREEMAN.

I know they are often fo called; and indeed there is fo great a likenefs betwixt two of them, poetry and painting, that their fifter-hood will be readily allowed: but betwixt mufick and painting there is no likenefs at all; and I am apt to fufpect that mufick paffes for the fifter of poetry, rather from their being often feen in company, than from any refemblance they bear to each other. For this reafon, when I examine how far tafte is concerned in thefe arts, I fhall confider mufick by itfelf. But either the diftinction betwixt tafte and judgment, which I gave your Lordfhip fome time ago, is falfe,

or

or elſe taſte is totally excluded from being
a determiner in works of art, and muſt leave
that taſk for judgment to perform. An
art has been thus defined by one of the moſt
ſagacious of the antients, *a ſyſtem of rules
acquired by ſtudy, and reduced to practice,
for ſome uſeful purpoſe*. Now wherever there
is a rule or rules, by which any work is
ſuppoſed to be conducted, that rule, being known, muſt ſerve equally for a ſtandard to thoſe who would determine with propriety concerning its merit or degree of excellence. An art, then, and whatever pretends to a ſtandard, is an object of judgment
and not of taſte. As to muſick, it is certainly an art, ſo far as geometry is concerned
in it; but as the mathematical part of muſick is totally unknown to 999 in a thouſand
of thoſe who ſet up for connoiſſeurs in muſick,
including the performers, we may venture
to ſay that it is, with regard to them, no art
at all. Theſe virtuoſos, therefore, have nothing but their own taſte, that is, their own
private liking, to ſet up for a ſtandard, or,
what is little more mathematical, the liking
which thoſe of their club, city, or nation have
acquired by habit, that is, by the daily repetition of a certain ſtrain of muſick. What
diſputes therefore happen upon that ſubject
muſt be no leſs abſurd, than when cookery
is the ſubject of controverſy. With regard

D 4

to

to the fifter arts of painting and poetry, the case is very different: for in these arts there is not only a standard, but one so level to the common sense of mankind, that the most ignorant are acquainted with it; and, if it is unknown or mistaken by any, it is by the half-learned, who from their own conceit, or a respect for the authority of coxcombs, have tried to undervalue common sense, in order to substitute something which they thought better, in its stead.

Lord MODISH.

There is no doubt, Colonel, that there are rules for poetry and painting, and that there have been many ingenious books written both in prose and verse concerning these rules. But I fancy they are not so universally known as you would have us believe.

Col. FREEMAN.

Pardon me, my Lord; I have reason to be convinced by a thousand experiments, that the leading principle of criticism in poetry and painting, and that of all the learned principles which is the most unexceptionably true, is known to the lowest and most illiterate of the people. Those experiments are easily made. Your Lordship has only to hide yourself behind the screen in your drawing-

room,

room, and order Mrs. Hannah to bring in
one of your tenant's daughters, and I will
venture to lay a wager that she shall be struck
with your picture by La Tour, and no less
with the view of your seat by Lambert, and
shall, fifty to one, express her approbation
by saying, they are *vastly natural*. When she
has said this, she has shewn that she knew
the proper standard, by which her approbation was to be directed, as much, at least,
as she would have done, if she had got Aristotle by heart and all his commentators. He
has defined those arts, *arts of imitation*, and
his definition, though often obscured and confounded by more modern connoisseurs, has
never been contradicted by any. The same
country girl, who applauds the exact representation of a man and a house which she
has seen, will, for the same reason, be charmed with Hogarth's march to Finchly, as that
is a representation, though not of persons, yet
of general manners and characters, with which
we may suppose her to be acquainted. And
if she is less struck with the historical pictures of distant ages and countries, though
equally well painted, it is not because her
critical standard is not equally applicable to
them, but because the subject and manners,
there meant to be represented, are to her unknown, and must pass with as little observation

tion and remark as a good portrait of a person whom she had never seen. In all this I see no pretension taste has to be consulted. It requires first eyes to see, and then judgment to compare the exhibited image with that of the absent object, which is stored up in the remembrance, and is plainly a reflective and compound operation of the mind. It is indeed so quick and instantaneous, that it often passes for a simple feeling or sentiment; and is sometimes mentioned as such by criticks of no mean reputation, for want of having considered the nature of the mental faculties with that accuracy which they deserved. The general standard of poetry is exactly the same, and equally obvious with that of painting; and any experiment you make in that art upon a farmer's daughter, will be found to have a like event. It is only middling poetry which the illiterate do not understand and admire; when it arrives at a supreme degree of excellence it is adapted to the lowest class; and though other poets might have their partisans amongst the critics, there is no question, but Homer was the delight of every cook-maid in Greece.

Lord MODISH.

What, and won't you allow good and bad in poetry to be distinguishable by taste upon any occasion?

Col.

Col. FREEMAN.

No, my Lord.

Lord MODISH.

Then, my dear Colonel, your fpeculations and your common language are very little confiftent: for you faid, no longer ago than this morning, upon glancing over fome madrigals which are publifhed in Rowe's edition of Shakefpear, that the people of that age had a wretched *tafte* in poetry.

Col. FREEMAN.

It is true, my Lord; and I own myfelf to blame in ufing a word upon any occafion, which, as appears by the converfation we have had, is applied to fo many different purpofes, as to be unfit for any. We have feen that it fometimes fignifies *the faculty of diftinguifhing things fimply and without comparifon;* fometimes *that which pleafes fimply;* fometimes *that which pleafes by particular habit,* but moft commonly, *that which pleafes by general habit,* or what is properly expreffed by the fingle word *fafhion.* In this laft fenfe it was, my Lord, that I underftood the word tafte, when I faid the tafte of poetry was very bad in England, about a century ago; although it

is

is certain no age ever more abounded with men of genius and ſtudy.

Lord MODISH.

Darker and darker, by Pluto! I fancied, Colonel, about half an hour ago, that I had got a little light into your ſyſtem, but now I don't ſee one glimpſe. You told us then, that poetry was an art, and the object of judgment, and now you give us to underſtand, that neither imagination, reading, nor reflection, for that I ſuppoſe you mean by genius and ſtudy, are able to keep it in the right road.

Col. FREEMAN.

It is but too true, my Lord; theſe things can avail but little in the conducting of poetry, if faſhion, or, as they pleaſe to call it, taſte, takes it into his head to miſlead her. And when, by the neglect of juſt principles, any nation has habitually acquired a liking or taſte to cookery that is unwholeſome, to architecture that is inconvenient, or to poetry that, inſtead of inſtruction, conveys no ideas, or, what is worſe, falſe ideas to the mind: we may ſay, with great propriety, that ſuch a nation has a vitiated or a bad taſte.

LORD

Lord MODISH.

But how could habit, for I perceive now a little what you mean, so soon pervert our writers as to lead them all together into the same sort of error, even at the very first appearance of poetry in England ?

Col. FREEMAN.

To come easily, my Lord, to the knowledge of this, it will be necessary, once more, to turn our eyes to what was doing in the ages which preceded this. In those days, when miraculous legends under the name of history, and the absurdest of metaphysicks by way of philosophy, composed almost the whole of learning; poetry, which ever shares the fate of history and philosophy, was likewise at the lowest ebb. Instead of representations of truth, and the real existence of things, it consisted only of relations in ryme of giants, winged horses, griffins, castles moated round with fire and brimstone, knights that killed ten or a dozen men by one blow, and hermits that raised as many from the dead by one prayer; with a thousand other lies, which, however monstrous and unentertaining they may appear to us, were to those people so correspondent to the ideas that had been early imposed by authority upon them, that they

2   ap-

appeared not only probable, but true: and
although this correspondence of ideas could
not be very striking, as it is impossible for
the idle chimeras of a writer's brain to be
exactly the same with those of his reader, yet
they ceased not, along with persuasion, to give
them some sort of amusement. This was the
state of the epic; and low as it might be,
was only to be found in the happier climates of Italy and the south of France. There
likewise they pretended to a sort of lyric poetry, under the name of sonnets and madrigals, which, being founded upon the metaphysical quibbling then in vogue, instead
of the truth of passion and sentiment, was
wholly made up of jugling expressions, that,
with much subtlety, kept up a seeming relation betwixt thoughts, in themselves, not
at all akin. A sort of writing, though called by some people to this day *wit*, much
inferior to fair punning; as it equally trifles
with the understanding, without the merit of
shaking the sides. The arts, however, by
the means I mentioned some time ago, began
to revive; but they did not all keep an
equal pace in their improvement. Though
history was soon brought, in Italy, to a great
degree of excellence, philosophy, still a stran-
ger to experiment, continued to be only a
less absurd sort of metaphysicks; and by
keeping trifling subtleties still in request,
likewise

likewife retarded the fympathetic improvement of poetry: while her fifter painting,
difdaining the flow, bungling, and deceitful
medium of words, foon fhone forth with
all the luftre of nature and truth. All, however, were equally admired by the nations
on this fide of the Alps, who, having fmall
pretenfions of their own, and aftonifhed with
the tranfcendent glory of Italy, received in-
difcriminately every thing that came from
thence as the model of perfection. In England, for caufes that are eafily affigned,
the art of painting never took root; but,
though none of our artifts were infpired with
the divine fpirit of Raphael and Corregio,
our poets were much the worfe for having
read Dante, Ariofto, and Petrarch; the imitation of whom they preferred to good fenfe
and the imitation of nature. From this caufe
proceeded the tedious allegories, as they call
them, of Spenfer, and the jingling and ftrain-
ed conceits of Sir Philip Sidney. Happily for
us there were no Italian models for tragedy;
elfe Shakefpear's Othello might have been
as poor as his fonnets; and yet, even in thefe
his moft unrivalled performances, the mode
is often feen to prevail over the genius and
reflection of that great 'poet. Soon after this
importation of Italian tafte, the power and
majefty of the Commons of England began
to fhew itfelf; and as the contefts concern-

in-

ing the liberty and rights of Chriftians had introduced a fpirit of enquiry into Europe, fo that fpirit was carried ftill farther in England, by a new conteft concerning the peculiar rights of Englifhmen. Along with liberty all manner of property was farther afcertained, and that exorbitant power reftrained, which had been exercifed by kings and priefts over the opinions and fentiments, as well as the goods, of the people. The pleafure that arifes from the difcovery of truth, and the juft relation of things, is one of the greateft and moft lafting which human nature is capable of; and fo ftrong it is that to ftifle and reprefs it requires no fmall degree of violence. But this being withdrawn, the natural defire again takes place, and always with fuccefs. So it happened in England, where learning went hand in hand with the conftitution in all its changes. As liberty and order grew, learning and juft fentiments flourifhed; as thofe degenerated into enthufiafm and anarchy, a like feaver fucceeded in the ftate of literature. It was madnefs, indeed, but it was of the vigorous fort, from whence much good was ftill to be expected. Accordingly, upon the return of a more fettled government at the Reftoration, when liberty was tempered by a certain degree of fixed fubordination, the fciences likewife took a more orderly and more polite

turn,

turn, without giving up any of that freedom which they had affumed. Party con-
troverfies loft much of their acrimony, and
men began to ufe the weapons and dexterity
which they had acquired in thefe contefts,
to more peaceable and more valuable purpofes. The Royal Society was founded, and thofe
hints which Sir Francis Bacon had given
with regard to experimental philofophy, were
diligently profecuted by the ingenious men of
that age ; fo that authority began, by little
and little, to give way to matter of fact,
fuppofition to certainty, and words to things.
But though in motion, ftill the progrefs of
poetry was flow. It is not enough for poets
to compofe in times of good fenfe: it is neceffary, in order to their writing well, that
they fhould be born in fuch times. The
ideas, which fill the infant imagination, will
always, more or lefs, keep poffeffion of it;
and are not eafily to be changed by later
knowledge and reflection. Notwithftanding
thefe new improvements in knowledge, the
gentle Waller ftill decked his Sachariffa, with
fuch unfcented gum-flowers as had adorned
the Laura of Petrarch; and ftill Milton thought
it proper to march his angels in a cubic pha-
lanx of well-bodied air, to attack as formidable a body of devils, who received them
with cannon in their hands, and puns in

E   their

their mouths. Intrepid devils, that knowing themselves to be immortal, dared to look death in the face, and to expose their unsubstantial forms to be pierced by the immaterial spears of their adversaries. What greater instance can be required of the detestable influence of romantic and scholastic jargon, than its producing such a hodgepodge in the brain of a man who has given such proofs upon other occasions, of a truly natural and noble genius. At last the Revolution, by establishing the rights of the several orders in the commonwealth upon a clear and solid basis, made way for an entire dissolution of that alliance, which had long been so stupidly and villainously cemented betwixt religion and politics. Metaphysics, now no longer necessary in support of opinions which were now no longer useful in the acquisition of power and riches, sunk by degrees into contempt; and Nature having at last shewn her true and beautiful face, poetry, from acting the part of a magic lanthorn teeming with monsters and chimeras, resumed her genuine province, like the camera obscura, of reflecting the things that are. The antient Greek and Roman poets being found to have conducted themselves more than any other, by this principle, the admiration of them encreased; and they, instead of the Italians, were chosen,

fen, to fet the fafhion, or, as we call it, to
form the tafte of writing. From them, and
from their miftrefs Nature, Prior, Addifon,
Pope, Swift, Parnel, and the reft of their
cotemporary bards, received the leaven, and
conveyed it, in their works, to the whole mafs
of the people. At this very day, when few
men take the trouble of becoming very learned, and fewer give to the public any proofs
of their poetic fire, the tafte acquired by the
laft age in certain kinds of poetry, ftill continues; and the moft infipid odes, that appear in the magazines, are better able to
ftand a critical difcuffion, than thofe that were
written by the brighteft wits a hundred years
ago.

Lord MODISH.

Then you efteem thofe magaziners to be
good critics, though but paultry poets; I
fhould think that required fomewhat more
learning than you feem willing to allow them.

Col. FREEMAN.

No more, my Lord, than it requires knowledge of geometry to navigate a fhip to
Jamaica; which, though it arifes from the
deepeft rules of fcience, is daily performed by thofe who never heard of Euclid, and
who are not capable to go through the eafieft

E 2   of

of his demonſtrations. Theſe arts, though
it coſt many ages of ſtudy to men of genius
to bring them to perfection, are, as far as
regards a limited practice, eaſily communi-
cated, by rote, to the greateſt dunce. A very
good pilot, who ſhould venture to diſpute
upon the principles of navigation, would
probably diſcover extreme ignorance; and the
ſame daily happens to men of mere taſte
whenever they meddle with criticiſm : ſo far
is good criticiſm from being a vulgar thing,
that even the taſte of the public, is ſtill
falſe in ſome kinds of poetry, particularly
in tragedy; under which auguſt title five
acts of language, ſuch as no mortal man ever
ſpoke, ſeldom fails of putting the profits
of three full houſes into the author's pocket.
A convincing proof that thoſe who frequent
the theatre judge of the elegance of a poem,
as they do of the cock of a hat, and have
nothing to influence them in their determination but mere taſte, or a feeling of what
is become by habit agreeable to them. Were
they to judge by the principles of art, their
deciſions would be equally juſt in all kinds of
writing.

Lord MODISH.

I hope you don't lay this likewiſe to the
charge of the poor Italians; for I don't
think

think we have ever been much troubled with
their tragedies.

Col. FREEMAN.

No, my Lord, it proceeds, I apprehend,
from an influence much more powerful and
popular, the example of our own Shakefpear; though, perhaps, the French tragedians have not been wanting with their
affiftance.

Lord MODISH.

This is fomewhat new from you, Colonel,
who ufed to fpeak with raptures of the genius
of Shakefpear.

Col. FREEMAN.

It is that very genius, my Lord, which
is the caufe of this evil; and we may fay
of it as Cato fays of Cæfar's virtue, *Curfe
on his genius, it has undone his Country.* Daz-
led by the fhining parts of fuch eminent perfonages, we are infenfibly led to admire and
to imitate, without diftinction, every thing
that belongs to them. What we cannot admire, at firft, or what we even difapprove,
we receive with difference, and ufe brings
us in time to be more or lefs pleafed with
it. All with juftice applaud when Hotfpur

E 3   gives

gives the contemptuous defcription of the courtier who came to demand his prifoners, fo full of that pride and vivacity which conftitute his character; but it was never yet known that the pit treated the actor with a hifs, or an *off, off, off,* when, in his relation of Mortimer's combat with Glendower, he fays

Three times they breath'd, and three times did they drink,
Upon agreement, of fwift Severn's flood,
Who then affrighted with their bloody looks,
Ran fearfully among the trembling reeds,
And hid his crifped head in the hollow bank,
Blood-ftained with thefe valiant combatants.

Lord MODISH.

There are, no doubt, falfe thoughts to be found in Shakefpear; but as it is equally certain they do not bear any proportion to thofe that are juft and noble, may not we reafonably fuppofe, that the imitation of him fhould be more ufeful than hurtful to our modern tragedians,

C<small>ol</small>. FREEMAN.

That is a happiness, my Lord, which never yet befell the imitators of any of the great
masters. To equal them in their beauties
they must draw them, as they did, from the
pure fountain of nature. Their faults they
may acquire from them, as they acquired
them from other faulty poets. Had not
Shakespear been perverted by wrong taste
and imitation, he could never have produced
such lines as those I have repeated. Nature
could never have pointed out to him that a
river was capable of cowardice, or that it was
consistent with the character of a gentleman,
such as Piercy, to say *the thing that was not.*
It is good rules alone that can save a poet
from such blunders, which taste is ever ready
to lead him into.

L<small>ord</small> MODISH.

Want of rules might indeed have been
the cause of those errors in Shakespear; but
that is not, surely, the case with the modern tragedians, either French or English.
They have had critics and rules in abundance.

C<small>ol</small>. FREEMAN.

No doubt they have, my Lord; but such
critics as are worse than none; and such
rules

rules as ferve to miflead their obfervers to fuch a degree, as to make them lefs fit to judge of poetry than nurfes and children: rules that are drawn from the works of authors, and not from common fenfe, or the general feelings of mankind. Afk one of thofe cricks for a reafon, and he gives you an authority; if you repeat your demand, it's ten to one but he fobs you off with one of thofe cramp words, that Lady Harriot has fuch a diflike to. As for inftance, if you afk Boffu, or any of the reft of the Ariftotelians, how the Severn came to be fo hen-hearted, as to turn tail and hide itfelf, on the fight of Glendower's and Mortimer's bloody faces, he will tell you that it is by a figure called profopopoia. This it is to underftand Greek. A foundheaded, though lefs learned crick, would probably have faid, that it was by a figure called nonfenfe.

Lord MODISH.

What, and do you defpife the poetics of Ariftotle, which have been revered through fo many ages?

Col. FREEMAN.

Far from it, my Lord; I look upon them as a moft valuable remnant of antient erudition;

tion; and, taking all circumstances into the
account, a prodigious proof of the genius of
the author. But I must own I despise those
moderns, who overlooking all the new disco-
veries, which time, perhaps, rather than human wit, has produced for them, do still, by
a most unholy bigotry, put their trust in his
infallibility. What would you think, Lady
Harriot, of a critick who could not conceive a
dramatic entertainment to subsist, with any degree of excellence, without a perpetual accom-
panyment of music?

Lady HARRIOT.

Indeed, Colonel, I should fancy that he had
never seen any thing but Italian operas.

Col. FREEMAN.

Your Ladyship's guess, is not far wide of
the mark; and yet, such is the sentiment of
the great Greek, of whose profound knowledge you must have read such wonders in
Pope, and the rest of the Belles-lettres-wri-
ters of your acquaintance. If any of our
London connoisseurs were to advise Garrick
to get Othello set to musick, by way of giving it more force and expression, it is not
likely he would be any more consulted in
theatrical matters. Not that I mean to de-
tract from the real merit of Aristotle. His

poetic

poetic fyftem will ever deferve the attention
of the learned, as it is founded upon the
folid bafis of experience ; but as this was
only the experience of what pleafed in his
age and country, it is too narrow a bafis to
erect fo lofty a pile upon, as an art of poetry.
Inftead of fearching into nature for fome univerfal principle of pleafure in that art, by which
he might in time form the tafte of his own,
and of every country, he, from what happened in his time to be their tafte, formed thofe
rules which have been tranfmitted to us, and
received as a work of deep philofophy, and
in which the whole myftery of writing was re-
vealed.

The more we examine into facts, the more
reafon we fhall have to be convinced, that tafte
ought never to be allowed to dictate in poetry ;
fince, when ever tafte happens to be good,
it is only the confequence, not the caufe of
good writing.   Judgment and rules, whofe
humble fervant and follower tafte ought to be,
are alone fit to decide, whether he is right or
wrong.

Lord MODISH.

So then, good tafte in poetry proceeds
from good poetry, good poetry from good
philofophy, and good philofophy from good
government.   A very curious genealogy.

Col.

Col. FREEMAN.

I have never yet, my Lord, met with any thing to convince me it was not a true one. And it is worth remarking, that the Italians, having recovered but little freedom in religion and government, are ftill extreamly behind their neighbours, the French and Englifh, in point of philofophy, and retain pretty much the fame tafte of poetry which they had two hundred years ago. Ariofto is ftill preferred to Taffo, and both to Homer; not only by the common run, but by thofe who fet up for criticks amongft them. As if a poet were to be efteemed excellent, in proportion as he departs from the imitation of nature, or the deficiency in that refpect were to be compenfated by a mufical gingle and flowing combination of fyllables.

In fhort, my Lord, altho' truth and falfehood, right and wrong, ufeful and prejudicial, proper and improper, will ever be univerfally the fame in themfelves, and their boundaries capable of being accurately diftinguifhed by human reafon; yet the taftes, feelings, and opinions of men, concerning any thing, muft never be admitted as evidence of its being in itfelf good or bad: Since a very few experiments may point out to us that thofe taftes, depending upon various tempers, accidents and

habits,

habits, are as numerous and various as the men, or fets of men, who are actuated by them. A variety the lefs to be argued againft, as it is manifeftly productive of general happinefs, and in fo great a degree that we may juftly pronounce any fociety of men in an unnatural ftate, whenever they are deprived of the benefits arifing from it. Whatever pleafes, pleafes; whether it be an ode of Horace, or a fermon of Whitfield; and whoever is made happy with either, he has my moft hearty congratulations, neither, were I willing to condemn him, fhould I know how to go about it. But if not content with this toleration, he perfifts in affirming that the one of thefe is in itfelf preferable to the other; I expect that he will lay afide his tafte, and give me his reafons. Upon fuch like occafions it has fometimes, too often, happened that in default of reafons, force, and terror have been applied, in order to produce an uniformity in thinking, and to render the tafte and opinion of the ftrongeft, the catholic, or univerfal. And then, woe! to the wretched fons of Adam!

Lady MODISH.

My Lord, are you for drinking tea under the oak, or fhall it be brought hither?

LORD

Lord MODISH.

I think, my dear, it will be pleaſanter out of doors this fine evening. Well, Colonel, I ſee this is your day; and that I am but ill prepared to be a champion for taſte. But, as Patroclus ſays to Hector, you have not long to enjoy your triumph; for to-morrow I expect Jack Maggot. He, you know, is a great *dilettante*, and full of taſte to the brim; and I doubt not of ſeeing you brought to ſhame for the complication of hereſies you have uttered this afternoon.

Col. FREEMAN.

My Lord, I accept the challenge, and deſire only a clear ſtage. Allons.